MIRACLES
IN THE
MAKING

MIRACLES IN THE MAKING

Editor: Carolyn Wing Greenlee
Consultant: Linda Marie
Tech Support: Ron Doerksen

Cover design and photo: Dan Worley

ISBN
978-1-887400-72-5 (paperback)
978-1-887400-73-2 (kindle)
978-1-887400-74-9 (hardcover)

Earthen Vessel Productions
www.earthen.com

Contents

Acknowledgements

This book is the result of a team of people working together to bring to the public the actual stories of God's miraculous working in the hearts and lives of regular people who are believers in the ability of God to deliver them from dire circumstances that would otherwise lead to the loss of their lives.

Carolyn Wing Greenlee is the leader of this team. She is the one who heard my stories and believed that God would use them to encourage many others to believe that God would work miracles for them in their times of deep distress. As we prayed, it became clear to me that God really did want me to write of the miracles in our family, and families close to us. She extended herself to teach me creative writing, she read and readjusted my time line in the stories, and was also a mentor-on-call.

Dan Worley does the layout for the printing of the book, and provided the cover photograph. It is an actual picture of the cloud formation during one of the awful wildfires in their area. He is the technical support for Carolyn Greenlee.

Ron Doerksen is my technical support and kindly came to my aid many times in negotiating my way through the writing errors, and computer hiccups that stalled our progress from time to time. He was a great help to both Carolyn and me.

Family members were really helpful in relating their stories to me when I did not remember certain incidents, or was not present when things happened to them. They filled in a lot of details that I did not know about so that the final story was well rounded out for the reader.

My oldest son, Stephen, surprised me on my birthday with an updated computer that was much faster than the one I was working on. I am most grateful to him for his generosity.

My aunt, Mildred Bryans, was invaluable as a resource of information of the earliest days in our family. She and I were the last remaining family members of our generation. Sadly, she died midway through the writing of this book.

Earl Johnson, a missionary who worked closely with my Father, Percy Wills, on the West Coast of Vancouver Island, B.C., Canada, gave me permission to access much information from his own book, "Looking Astern," as well as his deceased wife's book, "Not Without Hope." Since I had never been on that mission field until 2008, their books were invaluable for details in the stories that I could never have known.

Roy Getman, is a fellow missionary in the same field as my father's. In 2008 when I visited his mission base he handed me three folders of writings my father had entrusted to him years earlier, with the statement, "You will know who to give them to." Without the information of my father's younger life they contained, neither this book, nor my earlier one, "Forging Ahead for God," could have been written.

Judy Inkster provided a critical piece of information that allowed me to bridge a time gap in one of the stories.

Linda Marie, MFT, kindly offered to proofread my stories. I am very grateful that she was available for that purpose.

These three books held much detail of winter storms, dates when certain events occurred, and other much needed data to complete some of the stories:

Forging Ahead For God, Darda Burkhart, Deep River Books, 2nd printing, 2014

Not Without Hope, Louise Johnson, Maple Lane Publishing, Canada, 1992

Looking Astern, Earl Johnson, copyright Earl Johnson, 2018

FOREWORD

"I will [solemnly] remember the deeds of the Lord;
Yes, I will [wholeheartedly] remember Your wonders of old.
I will meditate on all Your works
And thoughtfully consider all Your [great and wondrous] deeds." (Psalms 77:11-12 AMP)

George Müeller supported thousands of orphans in England in the 1800s, never telling a soul about his financial needs for their care. At the time, God was being considered obsolete; the Bible fairy tales; and the Age of Enlightenment the dawning of a new, liberated, educated, advanced civilization. Why did George Müeller choose to do what he did the way he did it? He said he wanted people to know God is real, and the proof would be a work that could not have come about any other way but by His own sovereign hand.

I was impressed by George Müeller but he lived long ago. Nobody I knew had ever attempted anything like that. Maybe that was for then, the ways of the old days. But then my friend, Dale Billester, started telling me stories of his grandfather's adventures on the perilous Pacific Northwest Coast ministering to the people struggling to survive in that harsh environment called The Graveyard of the Pacific. Dale told me his grandfather saw the need for a hospital, sought the Lord in prayer, and built Esperanza with no money for land, materials, supplies, or staff. God supplied it all. I was fascinated. Then, one day, Dale said his mother was coming to town, and wondered if I would like to meet her. People had been after her to write a book about her father's ministry and she didn't know how, but Dale knew I did. So we had lunch together and have been friends ever since.

For decades now, I have been involved with this family, seeing first-hand the blessings of early choices by families of faith on the lives of offspring to the sixth generation. There have been trials, severe emergencies, and a lot of prayer. There has been miraculous provision, timing, and the resilience that comes from going through horrible things in the company of Almighty God. You will read some of their stories in this book. I have had numerous occasions to pray with Darda and her grandson, Jason. All I can say is they pray with the authority and power that comes from having looked death in the face more than once, and found God faithful.

Darda once told me the supernatural Christian life is normal. "That's the way it's supposed to be," she said. She is living proof, and she witnessed quite a few of the miracles she tells about in these stories. So when she told me the normal Christian life is meant to be full of God's miraculous interventions, it changed my expectation of my own life in Christ. In the 1930s, Darda's father began doing what George Müeller did—letting God supply rather than bringing the work about by his zeal for Christ and sophisticated marketing skills.

Into this present world come stories from an eyewitness who has seen what God does in ways that can only be explained by supernatural interventions. Miracles are proof that God not only exists, He is personal and deeply cares about each human being. He can bring great good through us into the world around us if we are willing to hear His heart, align with His ways, and follow His lead into a life far beyond what we could ask or even think.

My prayer is that you will read these accounts with fresh eyes and an open heart, letting the Holy Spirit of God whisper into your innermost being, that you, too, are meant to live in close communion with the Lord of the Universe, bringing about what He has designed you to do in such a time as this. It's normal. It's what He intended for you all along. You are created for good works in Christ, talking with your Friend in prayer, seeking His will, bringing it to Earth, carrying His light into a dark and frightened world. May you join the great cloud of witnesses who see first-hand the evidence of God's loving, supernatural interventions in the trials, sorrows, and struggles of human life.

"O give thanks to the Lord, call upon His name; Make known His deeds among the people." (Psalms 105:1 AMP)

Carolyn Wing Greenlee, author
MIGHTY: Vision for the supernatural normal Christian life
Walking In His Way: Aligning with the God of the Universe

Dedication

I would like to dedicate this book to God, our heavenly Father. He is the One who appointed me to write this book, as well as the Originator of all things pertaining to the people, the events, and the placing of the events, and even some of the wording described therein.

1

WHEN GOD GIVES FAITH
TO MOVE MOUNTAINS

Percy grew up in a loving, godly family who lived in Victoria, B.C., the youngest of four children born to Frank and Sarah Ann Wills. He had a brother Archie, and two sisters, Bessie and Amy. The family attended a local Methodist church and every Sunday they attended the morning and evening services, as well as the Sunday School in the afternoon. Even with this religious background, Percy did not know that he could have a relationship with Jesus Christ as his Savior.

When WWI broke out he and his brother joined the army and spent time in the trenches in France during the battles. After the war they both returned home to Victoria, but Percy was disillusioned and discontented from seeing the way men attempted to solve their problems. He wanted to find something that he could do to help mankind, not destroy it. In that mindset, he got a job with the Soldier Civil Reestablishment Service in northern Alberta, but even that did not give him the new outlook on life that he hoped it would.

He and an army buddy decided to go on a trip looking for adventure and excitement. Maybe that would give him some insights that he was looking for. They made it only as far as Winnipeg, Manitoba. While in that city, he visited some family friends who invited him to church. Even though he had been brought up in church and heard the gospel countless times, in that service God got his attention, and he gave his heart to the Lord.

One day Percy was reading his Bible and came across Mark 5:19 (KJV), which said "Go home to thy friends, and tell them how great things the Lord has done for thee, and has had compassion on thee." He felt a distinct call from the Lord to do just that—go home, and tell his family what God had done for him

1

and for his call to become a missionary. Here in the Bible was the answer to his heart's search. He went back to Victoria, packed up his belongings, and with the blessings of his loved ones, headed out for northern Alberta where he had previously worked.

This was his first lesson in walking by faith. That is, when God says to do something, you immediately obey and take the first step, whatever it is. For Percy, it meant giving spiritual care and support to the people he had come to know in that prairie country.

He found a small shack to live in, and, with a pack on his back, started walking to farms or lumber camps to tell those he met how loving and gracious God really was. This area was not well populated, so he was walking miles, not city blocks. The farms had large acreage and farm houses were not close together.

He had a heart for the people in this area who knew of God but had no spiritual mentor who could minister to them. Percy began by going to the farm houses and other homes to get acquainted with the families to tell them of Jesus and pray with them. While he walked, he prayed about the needs he heard, he meditated on Scriptures, and planned the sermons he would be preaching. The little old school house would serve as a meeting place where the people he ministered to could gather on Sundays.

However, in the time it took to walk to his destinations, he realized the need of some kind of transportation that would give him more time for visitation. Percy describes the supply of his need this way:

"One day I started down the trail and the first farm I approached made me welcome. 'Why are you walking?' they asked. 'I have no horse,' I said. They took me to the barn and presented me with one.

"As I approached the next farm bareback on my pony, I was asked, 'Where do you keep your saddle? Are you afraid of wearing it out?' When the kind questioner learned that I had no saddle, he immediately produced one from the tack room, saying, 'It's an old one that nobody uses any more.'

"From that day on, in [Percy's] ministry with others, whether the need was for a horse, a car, a truck, a boat, or a plane, as soon as the workers would rise and start on the journey, transportation would be provided, and not only equipment, but the fuel to keep it going."

The day came when Percy's money was running low and his cupboard was almost empty. Winter lay ahead and he would need warm clothing to get through it. He asked God to provide some funds. Just then, there was a knock on his door. One of the farmers needed an extra man on his threshing crew and asked Percy if he would help him. Percy knew this was God's means of supplying his provisions and he accepted this offer as he quietly praised God.

In that northern climate summer is short but with long daylight hours. When the crops were ready every effort was made to bring in the harvest quickly. Every minute was utilized, and the men worked tirelessly to feed the ripened grain into the threshing machine. It was very hard work—backbreaking labor. Percy was very strong, but by the fourth day he could hardly move. Rain came the next day and the respite enabled him to recoup his energy.

As the summer progressed Percy worked eagerly with the other men, sometimes on into the night that was lighted by straw stacks set ablaze to enable the men to see what they were doing. It was essential to get the harvest completed before the weather changed.

At the end of the summer when the harvest was in, the men collected their pay which was eight dollars a day. Percy planned to send away for the warm winter clothes he would sorely need. Before he could do that, a salesman came into the camp to take orders for a heavy sheepskin-lined coat. As with others, Percy paid the man 45 dollars for his order.

When no coats arrived and the men realized they had been scammed, they called on the police to investigate. When they asked Percy if he had lost money too, he replied he hadn't. This may sound like a lie, but since Percy had previously committed himself and all he had to the Lord, he reasoned that the money he lost was God's money. If God wanted to take it that way, it was all right with him. From his earlier lessons of God supplying his needs, he firmly believed God would supply this one for warm clothes some other way.

One Saturday night while Percy was preparing his talk for the next day's service, there was a knock on his door. When he opened it, a man handed him a bulky package from a mail-order house.

Percy was very surprised and said that he did not order anything from this company. The man said that it was addressed to him so he should take it. A little confused, but excited too, Percy opened the parcel and drew in his breath. He pulled out a beautiful warm fur coat. He was astounded. He could not have afforded such a quality coat, and he certainly would never have ordered one. It was a revelation to him that God was true to His promise of provision, and his gratitude overflowed in praise to God. He knew he could base his trust in God for supplying his needs for the rest of his life.

In one of his writings, which were many, Percy wrote this when an unexpected provision came at just the right time:

"Time and time again when resources had dwindled and come to an end, God would provide. Time after time, discouraged, disappointed and blue, God would revive. Often when humbled by mistakes and made penitent by blunders, God would come in His loving way and show that He never forsakes.

"When I dedicated my life to God for home missionary activity, I had ten cents remaining from the disposal of my affairs. On the morning that I was to leave for a distant place, I prayed and asked for the need to be supplied for train fares and other incidentals. I felt strongly moved to go to the post office, although I had already cleared my new address through the depot. There was a letter which had been mislaid, and in the letter was a check for one hundred dollars. From that day on, it has been one succession of hand-to-mouth experiences—but it has proved to be from God's hand to my mouth."

Many people told Percy he had great faith. "No," he replied. "I just have faith in a great God." But his strong faith in God was a constant example to his fellow Christians of God's unending compassion and care for the needs of His children.

About a year later Percy was in Edmonton, Alberta. While there, he was asked to visit a woman who had broken her leg and was hospitalized. As he talked with her about the Lord, he asked if he could pray for her. She nodded a "Yes" and Percy said a very simple prayer asking God for His healing hand. When he looked up, the woman was very alert. She shouted, "I'm healed. I'm healed." She called in the nurse and insisted that her cast should be removed. She said she was healed, and she was going to go home. Even the doctor could not dissuade her, and he finally acquiesced and her cast was taken off. The woman got dressed and went home.

Percy went quietly on his way, but the next night, the woman and her daughter were in his meeting. He spoke to them after the meeting, not knowing God had arranged the events for His own purposes.

That evening Percy was praying about his day and what God had in store for him the next day. God spoke to him in that quiet time, informing him that the woman's daughter, Margarette, was to be his wife. Well, that was a shocking thought. He had not the slightest thought of marriage. He had no regular income, and his dwelling place was not adequate for a couple. His ministry was in an area where she would be left alone for hours at a time without anyone nearby whom she knew. Yet, the more he prayed about it, the stronger that conviction became.

Once he was assured that this was really God's will, Percy visited the young woman at home and asked her to be his wife. She was as startled as he had been, for they had just met and she knew nothing about him other than what he had told them, though she did say she would pray about it. He returned to his mission field to prepare for the wedding. He was so at peace while he resumed visiting his parishioners. They were all congratulating him, wishing him well, and eager to meet his wife when they returned. One couple offered one of the rooms in their home for Percy and Margarette's abode. That was a blessing, for it meant Margarette would be with people while he was gone.

A few weeks later Margarette sent Percy a telegram that he was all she could think about. She would marry him. His heart swelled with this response knowing that God had put a love in each heart for the other. This would not be a small, quiet wedding. Margarette and her mother Maggie were well known in their church, and there would be many friends invited to the nuptials.

Percy left the North Country to go to Edmonton for his wedding with $15 in his pocket, which his parishioners had given him, along with their best wishes. He expected the sum would be sufficient to buy the ring and to pay for the marriage license and the minister. But when he arrived in the city, he discovered that his $15 would not cover his requirements. The license cost $7.50, the ring cost $8.50. On top of that, the minister's wife told him he needed a new suit. She reminded him that he was marrying one of the finest women in Edmonton.

Percy went back to his room that night penniless and greatly distressed. What was he going to do? He had no more money and didn't know where he could get some right away. He did what he always did when he faced a seemingly hopeless situation. He spent the night on his knees, struggling with his own worries about the overwhelming needs and his inability to meet them, till the peace of God filled his heart.

The next day Percy and Margarette went shopping to pick up the ring, license and suit. Some mail came as they were leaving the house. The postman handed them two letters for Percy and each one had a check in it. One of the checks was from 'O.H.M.S." (On His Majesty's Service). It contained an official government check for $100, a large amount in those days. The other was from his family in Victoria and the check was for $25 as a wedding gift. The total was more than enough to cover all the expenses he had.

Percy's heart leaped with praises to God for this prompt answer to his prayer. It was also an encouragement to Margarette to see how faithful God would be in supplying their needs. Many times over the course of their marriage they would find God faithful in similar ways. Sometimes, God waits until the last minute, but He is always right on time—His time.

The couple was so ecstatic and happy they almost danced their way to town to complete their shopping, praising God all the way. With ample money they paid for the ring, license, and new suit. They ordered flowers and bought gifts for the wedding attendants. They felt the day's shopping was most successful.

That night, Percy and Margarette became Mr. and Mrs. Percy Wills, under the blessing of the pastor and many friends in attendance. Their marriage lasted through many ups and downs, hopes and tears, joys and sorrows, for almost 50 years.

This was another lesson of God's leading Percy even in such a personal matter as important as one's life partner. God has a plan for each of our lives according to Psalm 139:13–16. He designs each baby with the abilities that he or she will need to carry out the purposes God has in His mind for that special one. When we become a child of God, we have the privilege of following His plan that will lead us to the fulfillment of His destiny for us.

Percy and Margarette moved into their new home, a rented room that Percy had arranged for prior to their wedding. Margarette was a strong spiritual support for Percy in his mission work. But the situation changed when she became pregnant with their first child. The doctor found that she had an overactive thyroid gland and he was concerned about her heart being affected. They decided to move back to Edmonton where she could have better medical care than was available where they were. I don't know whether they lived with her mother Maggie, her brother John and baby sister Mildred, or if they rented a small apartment.

Their son Francis (Frank) was born the next year, much to the delight and rejoicing of family and friends. After his birth the doctor spoke to them about Margarette's condition and said that she should not have any more children because the strain on her heart would be quite a risk.

At that time, and I am not sure why, though it may have been the need for a regular income, Percy decided to step back from missionary work and took a job in an insurance agency. He did well in the business field, but his heart was troubled at the same time.

Little Frank continued to grow and develop into a handsome little boy. He had dark, curly hair, brown eyes, and long eyelashes. He was happy and playful, obedient and quick to learn.

I'm told when Frank was about four years old, he became quite ill with something akin to what we now know as Polio. He was listless and lethargic, and it seemed his legs didn't work as they should. The doctor did not seem to have any medicine that brought relief. Percy and Margarette were getting desperate for his life. Friends and family were praying deeply for God's intervention and healing but nothing changed in his condition.

That was when Percy remembered God's call on his life. He fell on his knees and humbly confessed his sin. He prayed that if God would heal Frank, he would leave his job and go back into ministry. God graciously answered that prayer. Almost immediately Frank began to improve until he was out of danger and completely back to normal.

Percy kept his part of the bargain and quit his job even though he had no idea how, or where, he would go to minister. His heart and mind were once more connected to a strong faith that God had a place for them somewhere. Margarette trusted God with him and encouraged him that God would lead them once again to a new field of ministry.

This next major change in Percy's life has always been a mystery to me, and I had no idea how he and his family left Edmonton, Canada, and started fresh in Auburn, Washington. It was just a few days ago that I received a probable answer, although I cannot document it due to the passage of time.

I was told that because Percy had no idea where to look for an opportunity, or opening, for a minister, he may have contacted the headquarters of the Assembly of God churches. They would have openings for new ministers to replace a pastor who moved on, or known of places where they wanted to start a new church. It may be that Percy was asked if he would go to Auburn to plant a new church. A small group of people there had made the request.

Regardless of whether this is the motivation behind their move, we know that our God is more than capable of connecting people He wants to work together. His ingenious ways of doing so are often a story in itself.

Percy and Margarette with little Frank arrived in Auburn eager to meet the ones who made the request for a pastor. At that time, Auburn was a farming community not far from Seattle, and those who welcomed Percy and Margarette were farmers. They became dear friends who gathered together in heart, soul, and purpose to start a church where God would be honored and people could come for spiritual connections with that same God.

It did not take long for them to get settled in the community. Once that was done, the small group of fewer than 10 people started planning the church. They probably could get help in doing this from the organization that assigned Percy to this project.

The group rented a small building so they could start meeting together on Sundays, and maybe midweek for a prayer service. Percy began teaching them the things of God that he had learned during his previous ministry. He determined to preach about Jesus and the Scriptures pertaining to Him. Soon other people in the area began to come to hear this new preacher. Apparently they liked his sermons because the church started to grow. It was not long before they needed a larger building, and so they prayed about this matter, and once again God heard and answered.

I'm told a lady who was interested in this work donated a plot of land for a church building. Work on the church started almost immediately. When their own work day ended, the men joined Percy to begin digging out the foundation. Slowly, but surely, the building took shape and when it was completed, a small group of people, including the charter members, held their first service with praises to God for this accomplishment.

The church continued to grow and flourish under Percy's teaching. As they grew spiritually, the Spirit of God was very present in their meetings. People got saved, and there were times when others were healed. The church is still alive today, though not as large.

After about five years as their beloved pastor, Percy and Margarette began to sense it was time for them to move on. Part of it was due to Percy being a Canadian citizen living in the United States. Although Margarette was raised in Canada, she was an American citizen, having been born in Oklahoma. There may have been some regulations in either country that pertained to this situation. The current green cards were not in existence in those days. I do remember something about a Canadian citizen living in the United States having to return to Canada every six months for a certain amount of time before he could go back to the U.S.

This matter became the subject of a lot of prayer, asking God what His plans were for them. They felt fulfilled in serving the people of their church, but lately there was just something in their spirits that did not fit quite right.

The answer to their prayers came in a letter inviting them to be missionaries with the Shantymen on the rugged west coast of Vancouver Island. Once again, they prayed, and God's answer led to their moving to Vancouver B.C.

Many miracles came about because of their obedience to the Lord, including the birth of their second child, who witnessed many of the marvelous works of God and has written a number of the astounding accounts that are recorded in this book.

The effectiveness of the ministry of Percy and Margarette Wills was based on the foundation of strong faith and much prayer, resulting in miracles that were an answer to a need, a problem, a trial, or even a crisis throughout the many years that Percy and Margarette walked in obedience to the Lord they loved so deeply. That legacy continues to this day, extending with grace and power through six generations of offspring who serve the Lord in their own walks of faith in the love of their Lord.

2

WHEN GOD BUILDS SOMETHING FROM NOTHING

In the year 1930, a young man, Percy Wills, received a letter that would drastically change his life and the life of his family, his wife Margarette, his son, Frank, and me, his baby daughter, Darda. The letter was an invitation to join the Shantymen's Christian Association (now SCA), as a missionary to the west coast of Vancouver Island, B.C., Canada.

At the time, Percy was pastoring a thriving church in Auburn, WA. Joining this missionary organization would mean moving his family to Canada, leaving an established church in order to minister to a new group of people who lived in a very isolated area. Both the new organization and the new people of the mission area were unknown to him. It would also mean changing from a monthly salary to learning to live by faith in God to supply his financial needs above the small stipend he would receive from the mission. (An early record reports that the salary of a missionary couple was $12 dollars a month).

After much prayer, thought, and discussion with Margarette, Percy was led of God to accept the offer. He spoke to his congregation and told them of this move. There were sad partings because he was their pastor and had founded the church, but they realized that this move was of God. With tearful prayers and help in moving, they said their goodbyes to Percy and Margarette.

Our family moved to Vancouver, B.C., to live with Margarette's family who had a home there. We didn't know anyone in that city and since I was a new baby in the family, Mother would have help caring for me and my brother Frank. Percy would be gone for weeks at a time, visiting his territory and getting to know the people who were scattered over 300 miles of coastline edged by the Pacific Ocean.

Percy's first trip on the southern coast of Vancouver Island was in a rented Indian dugout canoe with two sets of oars, accompanied by a friend and an Indian guide who knew the territory. Percy and his friend rowed while the guide helped navigate them through the unfamiliar territory. They visited several small villages during the day and introduced themselves to the residents. At night they camped under a tarp. On that trip, Percy saw the dire needs of these isolated peoples for fellowship, for comfort, for spiritual support, and for medical help.

When the trip ended they had to pay the rent for the canoe. Percy had no money, but he had a very good sheath knife that the owner accepted in trade. That was one of Percy's first lessons that God would really supply, from whatever source, his present and future needs for his missionary work.

The next summer, the manager of a fishing company who had heard Percy speak about his work, offered the use of any of the fleet of fishing boats at the dock. Percy chose a 50-footer so they could travel farther north on the coast. He also chose the crew, which included an engineer, a couple of men who were local board members of the mission, and a retired missionary doctor.

That summer, Percy and his crew visited virtually every inlet and bay from Victoria to Kyuquot Sound, encountering poverty on every level. The doctor treated almost 300 people, doing dentistry as well as treating medical problems. To the most needy, they gave out used clothing, and they held services at every cannery and logging camp. Surprisingly, they found that hunger for the Word of God was even greater than they had anticipated.

The board members who were on that trip realized the need for the mission to have their own boat. They also realized that God would have to provide the funds not only to build it, but also the expenses of maintaining it in the future. They brought that need to their prayer group who met weekly and to the churches in Victoria. This was during the Great Depression when money was scarce. However, money began to come to the local board and construction of a boat began.

One donor was a young boy who heard Percy speak. He went home and got a jar, labeled it "for a Shantyman boat," put his two pennies in it and asked the Lord to bless his pennies. When his mother found out what he was doing, she told others. The two pennies caught the imagination of people and they started to give until the jar was full. When the money was counted, it amounted to 300 dollars. This gift started the building of the boat that would be named Messenger II. When it was completed, all the bills had been paid and there was still 400 dollars in the bank account. In 1934, the boat was dedicated and commissioned for the work with much praise and gratitude to the Lord.

Now that the mission had its own boat, Percy took the helm and began visiting along more of the coastline. In his heart was a strong desire to find a suitable piece of land where a hospital could be built. That desire had been increasing ever since he took that first trip in the rented canoe and saw the great medical needs. There were no medical facilities of any kind on that side of the island. The local jobs were in logging, fishing, and canneries, and even some mining, so the possibilities, or more likely, the probabilities, of accidents were high. There was also the need of maternity and birthing help and the special needs that older people tended to have. There was no minister to help them when a loved one died. They would have to build the coffin, dig the grave, and carry their grief alone.

One day in 1937, Percy was searching for a parcel of land for a hospital. In the Esperanza Inlet where it was protected from the storms lashing the western coast, he found exactly what he was looking for. He anchored the Messenger II, and took to the skiff for a closer look. It was perfect. It was right on the water and the ground was fairly level with enough space where several buildings could be erected. There was a southern exposure that would receive all the sunlight there would ever be. It had a stream of pure water flowing through it. And there were a few small communities and logging and fishing camps nearby so it was not totally isolated. The major difficulty was that it was virgin land that backed up to a rocky area and would have to be cleared.

Percy quickly contacted his associate, Dr. Herman A. McLean, to tell him about his finding and to invite him to join him to see the place where they would build the hospital. Doc was now part of the mission staff but he had not yet joined Percy to begin the work.

Dr. McLean was a tall, solidly built, likable man who carried a presence with him. He spoke quietly and easily, but he meant what he said and you knew you could trust his words. He also had quite a sense of humor that came out from time to time.

The first thing Doc had to settle was where his wife Marion and their five children could stay for the time he would be gone. He prayed strongly for a good place for them to live during this period. The answer came within hours. A family in Sidney, near Victoria, was going away for several months and wanted someone to live in their home for that length of time. Word was passed on to Percy, and he and Doc traveled to Sidney to look over the house. It proved to be abundantly suitable for what they needed, so the family joyfully moved in. Another answer to prayer that provided a comfortable setting without cost to them.

While they were in Victoria, Percy and the McLean family joined the weekly prayer meeting to give them a report on what they had accomplished so far. The group took on this need, supplying backup in seeking the Lord to provide adequate funds for all aspects of building, purchasing, and maintaining the property.

When Percy and Doc in Messenger II got back to the property again, they spent some time in prayer asking God for guidance in planning for the next step in building, and that He would provide everything needed, e.g. lumber, tools, nails, screws, etc. They decided to start building right away in order to benefit from the longer summer days. The mission did not own the land, nor was there enough money for it in the bank. But Percy and Doc felt the urgency to start building because construction would have to stop when the rains came. As for owning the land, they decided to put the building on skids so that it could be moved off if the application for ownership was denied.

The Lord had His hand in this effort also. Across the bay was a small sawmill where all the lumber needed was available. Doc and Percy sailed over to see how much lumber they would need for a small building, about 14 by 32 feet. The foreman they met there was angry and had a terrible hangover from the previous night's binge. When they asked about the cost he snarled, asking what they were building, and Percy replied they were going to build a mission hospital. Well, that set the foreman off on a wild rant that "They don't want no mission here!" Percy and Doc were not shocked because they were quite aware that the liquor industry had a heavy hold on the men and did not want any spiritual movement to disturb their business. Percy quietly replied, "I didn't ask you if you were interested in mission hospitals, I just asked you for the price of the lumber." The foreman stumbled off saying that he would get the manager for them.

The manager came out and asked, "What do you want the lumber for?" When the two men told him, he asked, "How soon do you want to start?" "Right away" they said. The manager wanted to get rid of them too, so he said, "I'll give you the lumber free if you get it out of here this morning."

The glee of victory of what God had just done gave Percy and Doc renewed energy, They dumped all the lumber they needed in the bay, lashing it into bundles. It didn't take them long and the Messenger II towed the lumber back to the new site to unload it on the land. They were full of praises to God for this new experience of His full provision and this evidence that He really would supply all their needs according to His riches, not theirs.

Now a whole new set of problems faced them. It was virgin land with lots of trees and bushes on it. You can't build anything until the land is prepared for that work. The need to clear the site was way beyond the ability of these two men, regardless of how strong they were, or how much they wanted to do it. What to do? Once more God stepped in.

Volunteer labor came from men who were out of work at the nearby fishing camp. In appreciation for their help, Doc promised to pay for their meals at the bunkhouse when the summer was over. The men were glad to hear this, for they were not getting paid at the time. Other volunteers were some of the Indian men who came to help clear the land and take part in working on the buildings. Later, when the buildings were completed, some of the Indian women came over to help Marion with all her duties, even to babysitting little Garth. These gifts from the Indian people helped to forge an ongoing, real bond of friendship and respect between them.

We need to realize that, in the 1930s, much of the labor was manual. For instance, loggers who cut down big, old trees had to do it with long, two-handled saws with one man at each handle. They pulled back and forth until the tree fell. They did have some heavy equipment machines to haul the trees out to the trucks that took them to the mill, but the volunteers were used to heavy work and were not daunted in view of the labor needed to get the land ready for building. They were burly, muscled men who could work for hours at a time without a break.

By August of that year, the land was cleared and the building was almost completed. Doc turned his energies to getting equipment and furnishings. Another pressing need was for nurses to assist in the hospital operation.

Just before Percy left in the Messenger II, Doc talked to him about this need, suggesting that he write to some nurses who might be interested in signing on to this mission endeavor. He was surprised when Percy said, "No, Doc. God knows the nurses He wants up here. He'll send them."

That Fall, a fully trained nurse applied to work in the new hospital. A friend of hers, who was also a nurse, felt God calling her to the coast and the two of them arrived together. A young man had also heard of this outpost hospital and wanted to join it. The three of them arrived on the same boat. This again, was another lesson to Doc that God was covering every aspect of the ongoing needs of the fulfilling of this dream He had given them.

As for supplies, God provided for that as well. It was not uncommon for the supply trucks to have unloaded their cargo and be about to leave the dock just as someone came with money to pay the bills. Both Percy and Doc walked closely with God and were led daily by the Spirit. They expected God to provide for them.

In September, Doc contacted his wife and said it was time for them to join him in Esperanza. The family had been waiting for this day to come, and eagerly they packed up. Friends helped them with this task, and the neighbors added their good-byes. Members of the Shantymen's Prayer Group met them at the ship in Victoria, helping them get all their luggage on board the S. S. Princess Maquinna, adding their farewells and prayers for God's protection on the trip and His grace for facing the unknown future.

After two days at sea, the ship docked at Nootka, where there was a large cannery, a hotel and several nice-looking homes along the hillside. A messenger came on board to give Marion a note from Doc. It said that she would have to get off there and stay at the hotel because a place was not ready for them yet. She was quite surprised at this and wondered how they could live in a hotel, yet she was grateful to God for this provision until the hospital was completed and the family could be all together again.

The owner of the hotel was very accommodating. He put Doc's family in a large upstairs room and made laundry and kitchen privileges available to them. The children loved to watch the fishing boats unload their catch of fish at the dock and listen to the tales the fishermen would tell them.

A reason for the delay in moving on to Esperanza was that two rooms were to be added to the hospital building for the family's home. When they were completed Marion, with their five children, Max, Don, Shirley, Bruce, and baby Garth transferred their belongings to their new home.

October days followed and on November 1st, the hospital was ready for patients. That evening, Doc was outside working in the last bit of light. He heard a boat approaching and the men in it yelled, "Is there a doctor here?"

Doc replied, "I am the doctor. What do you need?"

"We've got a man on board nearly dead!"

"Bring him in!" This was Doc's first patient on the very day God had promised that the hospital would open.

The patient was a logger. Under his arm was a large swollen gland full of poison that would take his life if immediate surgery was not done. Doc got ready and made a wire mask for the anesthetic, and said one of the men would have to hold it for the patient. Since there was no electricity, Doc relied on a strong light on his head lamp by which he was able to lance the gland to clear it, and finish the surgery. It was nearly midnight when the patient was put to bed to rest and recuperate.

As it does in small places, word soon got around about the logger, his surgery, and that the doctor really knew what he was doing. After that, people became more friendly toward Doc. His reputation grew. Men started coming to him from far and near, knowing that they had a "real" doctor who could help them even in severe situations.

Now that the hospital was "up and running," Doc sent a message to his wife and family to come on the next boat that would take them. The message said that the place was ready and he couldn't wait to see them after all these months. Hurriedly they all got their things together, thanked those who had been such a help to them, and found a fish packer ship that was headed to that area.

The two days on the ship seemed to pass so slowly as their excitement grew. Marion and the children were eager to see their new home with Dad standing on the shore waving to them. When the captain turned the ship into the Hecate channel they all stood at the railing scanning both sides of the water, the children vying to see who would be the first to spot the hospital. A short time later the captain announced, "This is Esperanza."

When they saw what was to be their new home for the foreseeable future, things got really quiet. It was nothing like what they expected. They didn't know how to react. They couldn't have imagined such a dismal scene. It was only two small shacks. Surrounding the shacks was dense underbrush; towering above the underbrush were enormous fir and hemlock trees with the steep, rock-faced mountains. The scenery was stunning, but scenery doesn't help clear the land.

We can understand their shock at the sudden change of living conditions. No electricity—just kerosene lanterns. The only running water was the stream. No telephone, just radio communication. The heating system was the wood stove, for which all the wood would have to be cut by hand. This was November, heading into the dead of winter. The one good thing about that was they wouldn't have to worry about refrigeration because the weather would be cold and damp. Add to all that, this was a hospital. How would they keep necessary things sterile? Doc was very meticulous about that even in those primitive conditions. How will they do laundry for the seven of them, plus the patients? Rain or shine, all the water had to be brought from the stream, and then the laundry scrubbed on a wash board. It was a really laborious, ongoing task.

How could they cope in this situation so foreign to them? They would have to trust God for every little and big thing, as they began living a family life again. They were starting from a most primitive situation, where everyone would have to work very hard.

All the provisions they ordered would have to come by the Princess Maquinna that served the coast on a regular ten day schedule. The McLeans would have to bake their own bread, and canned goods provided their milk, vegetables, fruits, and some meat products.

Marion McLean really felt the loneliness deeply and prayer became her lifeline for strength to face the daily tasks. She knew that when her husband had asked to be sent to the hardest place on the west coast, God had answered that prayer. Yet she determined to be a partner with him in a place of such difficulty. The children had to work as hard as the parents to keep up with the demands that faced them all. There was no time for play—only more work.

The two older boys, Max and Don, had the task of rowing the little boat from their beach to the dock at CeePeeCee, a mile away, to pick up the mail and supplies from the Princess Maquinna, load it in their boat and then row back to their beach, sometimes in stormy weather. Then they would beach the boat, unload the heavy sacks of provisions and mail, and carry it all to a shed where the provisions could be stored out of the rain. They were ages 12 and 11 doing a man's work. They learned to use an ax very well, since they cut up all the wood for the stove. Occasionally, a logger would come over to help with cutting some trees and brush.

Shirley helped her mother and also had some assignments in the hospital. She enjoyed the part of serving tea or coffee to the patients. Every once in a while, she would apply analgesic balm or hot foments to the patients with sore muscles. That may have been the reason she eventually became a nurse in the same hospital.

Hardly had the family settled in and learned how to handle all the chores, than the next test reared its ugly head. Percy was in Port Alberni at that time and saw the Princess Maquinna at the dock. He decided to visit it in the evening. His friend Shorty was a passenger. Shorty told him the provincial land inspector was on board with instructions to sell the government lands at Zeballos, a mining town just north of Esperanza, and Esperanza itself. The hospital was on lot 2, and the ministry did not have ownership, although an application had been made.

Percy wrote a hurried note to Doc to go up to Zeballos and buy the land. He would go on the Maquinna that was headed to that destination. The only problem, and it was a big one, was that there was no money to pay the two hundred dollar sale price. Percy wondered, *How will God work this one out?* That night Percy was on his knees praying that God would provide the needed funds to secure the land, that the hospital might not only be safe, but could expand to a greater degree in the coming months and years.

In the morning, Percy called an old friend in the town who had been a surveyor in the past to tell him about the hospital. His friend offered to loan him the money to buy the land, but Percy said, "No, thank you. This is a time when God Himself will have to deliver us from this extremity." The surveyor suggested they check with a lawyer, to whom they told the entire story about the land being put on sale. The man listened intently to them, thought a moment, then turned to Percy and asked, "What were you doing this morning before you came?" Percy said he had been chopping wood at the Stranger's Rest, a place to house the homeless in town. The lawyer then said with a chuckle, "You go back to chopping wood—and don't worry." So Percy went back to chopping wood, and wondered what the lawyer had in mind. He thought back on what had been said in the interview, but couldn't come to any conclusion.

Not long after, Percy received a wire from the Minister of Lands in Victoria. The message was short, but very relieving. It read, "I have instructed our inspector to withdraw Lot 2 from the land sale."

What a relief! God worked so quickly. Percy's heart soared in praise to God that the hospital was now on safe grounds.

The rest of the story is surprising in a different way, but just as wonderful, for on the Maquinna the surveyor was nonplussed with the wire. He had worked at this job for thirty-five years, and had never seen a piece of land put up for sale to be taken off the list. It didn't make sense to him at all. He was disgruntled by this strange wire.

When the Macquinna docked at CeePeeCee, just south of, and on the same side of the channel as Esperanza, Doc picked up his mail. He started opening it. Every letter had a check in it. He quickly added them up and was shocked to find the total was $310.00! He was electrified! He could buy the land outright. The hospital was saved! So he practically ran to the inspector, waved all the checks in front of him, and said, "I'll buy the land right now, before it goes on the auction block."

The inspector was stunned to see how this whole situation turned out. He had been put off by the land being taken off the list, and now, here was this doctor with the cash in hand. He had no recourse but to help him buy the land. His whole demeanor changed and he decided to work with him. He even assisted him in getting a choice building site in Zeballos for an outpost in the future. Then he arranged that the Esperanza land be leased for a twenty-one year period at the low price of one dollar a year. Another marvelous intervention of God, proving that this project was of His design.

How is that for an example of God working miracles in such a short time. He had each person involved in the whole scheme right where they needed to be so that His whole purpose was carried out seamlessly. God can do the same for any child of God dealing with a complex problem.

At last the hospital was on solid ground, so to speak. The two buildings now fully in use meant that more buildings were required. Where would the nurses that God sent stay? They needed a dock for the boat God would provide, and a boat house where any needed repairs, or maintenance work could be done out of the weather. Along with the nurses, God called a young man with mechanical ability to offer his services.

Not long after this Doc's friend Shorty, was going to Victoria and invited Doc to accompany him for free. The night before they left, Doc had a dream. In it, he saw himself standing outside the little hospital looking at money that was scattered on the ground. He began picking it up, and when he counted the value of the bills, it came to $1,037. Then he woke up.

The next day, Doc and Shorty arrived in Victoria and met Percy at a small gathering of Shantymen who were meeting to raise some money for the hospital. When the meeting ended, they presented Doc with $50.00. That was not bad for a small group during the Depression. The next day, an older woman phoned him where he was staying, and said she had attended last night's meeting. The Lord spoke to her and told her to give him the total amount in her savings account, which was $900.00. Wow! Doc thought. He had only been in town for a few hours, and here he had almost $1,000.00! Before he left town he went to visit old friends in Sidney, and they also wanted to help in funding the hospital. When he left, he counted up the amount of the gifts that were given and they amounted to $1,037.00. Exactly the amount he had dreamed about a few nights previously.

With that money, he purchased a small boat for the hospital work and named it "Dieu Donne," meaning "The gift of God," a very apt name under those circumstances. Besides the boat, he was able to purchase an X-ray machine and some other essential things for this new work. His heart was overflowing when he headed to Esperanza, realizing once more how faithful God was to His promises of support for the mission God had given him.

The patient load grew to the extent that in the summer of 1938, a second story was added to the "shack" hospital that provided more beds. One of the rooms was turned into a much-needed operating room. Even that did not suffice for long. The patient list was still growing and often the rooms were crowded to capacity. Something had to be done and discussion began about building a completely new hospital building.

A special blessing came that summer, when a 1,200-foot pipeline linked the stream and the hospital. Finally there was running water available in both the hospital and home. Max and Don danced around with glee that they did not have to continue the bucket brigade by hand any longer.

In the meantime, other medical help was available at a new hospital in Zeballos for the mine workers. Also, some of the logging mills were beginning to shut down, and the fishing season was over. This was perplexing and called for concentrated prayer whether or not to build a new hospital.

Just about that time, a letter came from the Shantymen's Headquarters in Toronto that held a gift—a check for $4,000 dollar for a new hospital. In those days the economy was coming out of the Depression, and such a gift was a very large amount of money. That was God's answer to their prayers and planning for building began in earnest.

The new hospital opened in August 1939, fully debt free. It had space for sixteen patients, along with an X-ray room, a large sitting room, also used as a chapel and two two-bed wards on the main floor. A kitchen and a large dining room completed that area. A unique hand-operated elevator made the transport of stretcher patients from one floor to the other very easy. The second floor held the doctor's office, a nursery, a dispensary for medicines and supplies, and a large, sunny operating room. Three two-bed wards on the second floor helped to accommodate more patients than the previous hospital.

In his new motorized boat, Doc was able to expand his practice beyond the grounds of the hospital. His big heart and loving nature led him to visit smaller villages up and down the coast, and take care of people with illnesses or other medical needs that did not require hospitalization. Wherever he went he would hold meetings to tell the people about the God Who gave His life for them so they could be saved. He was welcomed wherever he went and the people warmed to him and trusted him completely, because they knew he truly cared for them individually.

Finally, it was time for the McLean family to have a real home built specifically for them. It was a two story home with a large kitchen looking out on the channel and lots of big windows to let in bright light on sunny days. Three more children, Dorothea, Lois, and Ruth added to the family, now numbering eight children. Doc sometimes quipped that he had "two and a half-dozen children."

Though they now lived and served in much more comfortable conditions, the McLeans never forgot those early days when the hospital was small and their labors arduous. Many works of faith are like that, and the joy that comes far exceeds the suffering, especially in the end when you stand before the King.

Sometimes God gives one of His children a big dream, so big they are afraid of it, but it won't leave them alone and they have to face it. Then they have to remember, and know down deep, that what God ordains, He is responsible to bring fully to pass, even though there will be opposition and problems along the way. The person's responsibility is to be obedient to Holy Spirit's leading, even when he does not understand how it fits in to his dream, and to trust God with his whole heart and mind that everything will work out in the end. And when his dream is out in the open, it will be proof that God Himself brought it to pass.

3

WHEN GOD GOES FISHING

This event happened during World War II in the city of Victoria, B.C., Canada. At that time, Canada was part of the British Empire. When Germany declared war on Europe on September 3, 1939, Canada also became involved on that same date. As with the U.S. in 1941, Canada had to quickly gear up its manufacturing to produce arms and equipment for the war. Men were immediately drafted to be trained before being shipped off to engage in the fighting. This is the time when Canada and the U.S. were just coming out of the Great Depression of the 1930s.

Here is a peek at the prices of some groceries in mid-May, 1930: Bread, 8 cents per loaf; milk, 56 cents per gallon; eggs, 49 cents per dozen. A car was $525, and gas was 25 cents per gallon. A stamp costs 2 cents each.

But before beginning the fishing story, some background information is necessary so the reader understands why this particular fishing trip was so necessary. After all, few of my readers, if any, would remember those days of eighty years ago, and what Canada went through during those six years of the war.

In brief, many foods were rationed and each person was given a ration book with a quota of stamps. When you shopped for groceries, you turned in the appropriate number of stamps. Foods such as dairy, meat, sugar, butter, etc., were restricted. Peanut butter became soy butter made with soy beans. I think we got extra stamps because we were feeding servicemen, so Dad had to keep records to prove the need for the extra stamps.

Gasoline was rationed, and the speed limit was set at 45 mph. Headlights had to be blacked out except for a small slit of light allowed to show through when driving at night. House windows had to have blackout curtains so no light could be seen from the outside.

The radio and newspapers were our only source of information about the war, the extent of it, and how Germany was swallowing up Europe so quickly. And then Japan bombed Pearl Harbor and we became involved in that arena also. The west coast of Canada became as vulnerable to attack from Japan as was the coast of the U.S. Since no one knew if any of the Japanese who lived in British Columbia were spies, the government decided to move all of the Japanese population who lived in the coastal cities to internment camps.

Men were drafted for the war and women started taking over some of the jobs that men had previously done. War Bonds were advertised and sold. Signs went up with messages and mottos such as, "Loose Lips Sink Ships." Groups sprang up to help in the war effort, such as women cutting up old sheets to make rolled bandages for the Red Cross.

Life was pretty tense for everyone, especially whenever we heard a loved one on the battlefield had been killed, or was MIA (missing in action).

My father, Percy Wills, left the mission field on the west coast of Vancouver Island to join the SACA (Soldier's and Airmen's Christian Association). Our family moved from Vancouver, B. C., to Victoria, B. C., for the purpose of opening a home there so there would be a place the servicemen could come when they had some time off-base.

Victoria was a military city. There were Army bases, the Navy had a drydock there, and the Air Force took over the airport. There was a great need for such a home when the city became host to all the servicemen who would have few places to spend off-base time other than the local bars.

My father rented a home that was perfect for that need. It was an imposing two-story home on a substantial corner lot with fruit trees and even a chicken coop. The house looked solidly built, yet was welcoming with a wide porch on two sides. A porch swing invited one or two to sit comfortably while chatting about things. It looked as if it was waiting for us to start moving in.

The house had big rooms on both floors—and a spacious kitchen where making meals for many people would be possible. It also had a sizable dining room that could seat a crowd, and often did. The living room had a large fireplace which promised a warm fire on a frosty night. Two wide windows had cushioned seats that could, and did, become beds when they were needed. Off the living room was a room that became an office, also available for extra seating. Even the entry hall would allow several people to stand and talk with ease and not be in the way of others passing through.

The second floor was made up of four good-sized bedrooms, a linen closet that would hold enough sheets and towels to change the cots more than once a week, and a bathroom with a sink and tub. The toilet was in a separate small room—just right for being available when the bathroom was in use, since it was the only bathroom.

Two of the bedrooms were for our family, one for my parents, and one for me alone. The other two rooms became dorm rooms with four cots in each so when some of the servicemen could stay overnight there was a place for them to sleep.

In the basement was a game room as large as the living room directly above it. In it was a pool table with all the necessary equipment. There was even another smaller room that could be useful also. The laundry equipment and tubs provided easy availability for the frequent need for fresh bedding and towels.

All in all, the Lord provided this house that was originally built for a large family, that was now going to be used for the glory of God for His larger family of servicemen from many parts of Canada and even Britain. Dad named the house "Emmaus," meaning "God with us." That name was perfect since the Lord would have to supply most of the needs to keep it open.

It did not take long for the servicemen and women to find the big house at 2024 Belmont Avenue. It was a place where they could be with a family—a "Mom and Pop," with me as their "kid sister." Those who had only a few hours could relax, read, play pool, and have a good meal, unlike what the military mess offered. If they had more time, they could stay overnight or for a few days. No money was charged for any of it. They were away from the war talk with a family, even if it wasn't their own.

Now you can see the reason for a fishing trip and the need for a good source of extra meat for the table.

My brother Frank had joined the Air Force hoping he could train to be a pilot. Unfortunately, his eyesight was not good enough. He was stationed at one of the air bases in the Prairie region. He was trained to be a radio operator, hoping for a chance to be a part of an airplane crew. Though that didn't happen, he understood the material so well that he was assigned to be an instructor.

When Frank's leave came up he told us he wanted to come home and asked if he could bring a buddy with him (Since I don't remember the buddy's name I will call him Norman). Dad said Norman would be most welcome during the days they were here.

When Frank and Norman arrived we welcomed them with hugs and great joy. It was so good to have them in our house and the four of us together once again. We hadn't seen Frank since our move to Victoria so there was a lot of catching up on his time in the Air Force, and getting acquainted with Norman.

Frank's leave time was short and he wanted to go fishing as soon as he could, so Dad called a friend in Nanaimo who had a fishing boat. When Dad told him what he wanted to do, his friend's reply was not what we wanted to hear. He said, "Oh, Percy, no one has caught any fish here for several days." When we heard that, we didn't know what to think. Shocked, we looked at each other with questions in our eyes. Is the trip off? Should we still go? We were confused, concerned, yet hopeful still that something would work out.

Because of our need of meat for the ministry to the servicemen and Frank's desire, it was arranged that the men could go out on the boat to the fishing grounds off shore. What a relief! We quit holding our breath, looked at each other with big smiles and laughed. We didn't have any fishing gear and the report from the experts was that no fish were biting, but we trusted the men would have the equipment they needed and we prayed, thanking God about the trip and asking Him to please do what He did for Peter, Andrew, James, and John, when they had spent all night fishing and caught nothing. Jesus told them to drop their nets on the other side of the boat and the fish raced into the nets.

The morning for the trip we got up quite early (because fish are up early), and were soon on our way. I tagged along with them for the drive north to the city of Nanaimo. Under normal conditions the trip would be about an hour, but with the speed limit at 45, it took almost two hours.

The scenery was so beautiful on that ride and a real eyeful for Norman to see the forested hills, the rocky places we passed by on the highway that went up a steep hill, the small towns we passed through. He was used to the large farms growing wheat and other staples with few hills to break the flat landscape at the horizon.

When we arrived we were warmly greeted by our friends (let's call him "Ted" and his wife "Marion"). A quick conversation provided information about the boat, equipment aboard, and pertinent things the men would need to know. Then Ted, Dad, Frank, and Norman clambered aboard, untied the boat and started the engine. The boat smoothly moved away from the dock, out into the Georgia Strait to the area where the fish usually were, but, as Ted had said, no one had caught anything for days.

The Lord must have told the fish to search and find Ted's boat because suddenly the fish were biting. Frank and Norman were so excited to see the large, silver salmon take the lures and the fishing poles bobbing up and down signaling fish on the hooks. Excitement took hold of them and praises and laughter flowed quickly as they began to reel in fish after fish after fish. It kept Percy and Ted busy getting the fish into the coolers, while Frank and Norman put new bait on their lines and got them back in the water expecting more fish to take the lures. And they did.

It did not take long until the coolers were full and it was time to head for the marina. All the men were as happy as could be. They spent the time going home talking over each and every catch, how the fish struggled on the lines, how they managed to get them on board, what kind of lures they used, and the ones that got away, although I don't think there were that many with the way God was working with them.

When the men arrived at the house, they filled the laundry tubs {which were much bigger than the kitchen sink} with fish—beautiful, glistening scales shining in the light. Best of all, they were all cleaned, ready to be prepared for the canning.

While the men were fishing, Marian, mother and I had been getting the canning jars ready, in faith preparing for the catch we had prayed for and trusted God to provide. The table was filled with empty jars, and I had wondered if God would really bring that much fish home to be processed. In my heart I was still praying and trusting that He would. Now all those salmon from that huge catch was there in plain view. It was so good to see them and know that God had heard our prayers. I remembered hearing what Ted said to Dad on the phone about not catching any fish for several days. I had been waiting in suspense to see if God would really come through. Would He do what He did for the disciples so long ago? Now I had proof that God does keep His promises to meet our every need. There were all those fish—lovely salmon that would feed the people for many meals.

Marion, Mother, and I spent the next several hours cutting up the fish, putting the pieces in the jars. The men joined us in this task since there was so much to do. Then as many jars as the pressure cooker could hold were processed for an hour to cook the meat and seal the lids. This was done until the last jars filled with the juicy salmon were taken out of the cooker.

There were so many jars that they filled several boxes. Joyfully the men put them in the trunk of our car. We said our goodbyes to the wonderful friends who had given of their time, boat, and equipment to help us in a time of real need. We prayed with them and thanked them profusely for all they had done for us.

The ride home was distinctly different from the one in the morning. That one was filled with hopeful uncertainty, but this one was gleeful. I sat in the back seat of the car between Frank and Norman, listening to the happy chatter among the others about the fishing and the excitement of it. I was musing over the work that the Lord had just done in answer to our prayers. He really did it! He really did it! What a lesson it was to me, to know that God really was faithful to answer prayers in times when nothing else could help.

It was late evening by the time we arrived at home, very tired, but extremely grateful to the Lord for His great provision that would give us extra food for many a day. It would also be a taste treat for those men who came from central Canada who may not have had fresh salmon available before.

Whenever salmon was on the dinner menu for the guests at the Belmont house, we told the story of the miraculous catch.

Again, the story brought about expressions of amazement, praise and thanksgiving to God for such provision in an unexpected way.

Today, our war is mainly a spiritual one—God's armies vs. the armies of evil who have taken over more territory than we are aware of. Our prayers are deep and heartfelt, trusting that God will overcome the enemy of our souls. Uncertainty hangs in the air. Will God come through this time? The economy is uncertain—Can I pay my bills this month? Will I have enough food in case the shortages last? Will my loved ones recover from the current viruses? These questions are on most minds, because we have no clear answers from the biased media.

Just as God provided fish for our necessary food so many years ago, today He will provide every need we have according to His promises. Only our trust in God will bring us through to a strong faith in His ongoing care, fulfilling His promises to us, His children. As we determine to keep close to our Savior He will instruct us and teach in the way we should go, and will guide us with His eye. (Psalm 32:8)

As someone once said, "Read the end of the Book. We Win!"

4

WHEN GOD STRETCHES YOUR DINNER PLANS

It was the very last Christmas holiday we would have at Emmaeus, the big old house on Belmont Avenue. For six years, this house had been a haven for servicemen and women. It was a place where they could find peace and be included in a family and its activities, rather than roaming around the city looking for something to do when off base.

In one way it was sad, because we knew we probably would not see these wonderful servicemen and women again. Some of the expected guests were stationed at the military bases in Victoria, adding to our family. Some were friends, but I can't say for sure who was there. After all, that's 70 years ago.

We expected to have 25 people for the New Year's Day feast. The menu included a large roast beef with mashed potatoes, good brown gravy, vegetables and dessert. The day before the holiday, Dad and Mother were in the kitchen preparing the vegetables and I was setting the tables when the doorbell rang. When Dad opened the door, a large paper sack was thrust into his hands. It contained a huge turkey, which someone had sent as a surprise. Dad took it into the kitchen and showed it to Mother. They wondered who had sent it and, more than that, what God was up to. Just then the phone rang, and Dad and Mother soon received their answer. Some China Inland Missionaries who had recently been released from a Japanese prison camp were on board an old tramp steamer that had anchored off shore. It was so derelict that it was a wonder it had made the journey across the Pacific Ocean and was still afloat. The crew had gone ashore for the holiday, but the missionaries were left alone on board.

The caller wanted to know if Dad could do something for them. Dad said that he would. Immediately, he called the Immigration

31

authorities, some of whom he knew personally, to see what could be done to bring the group to Victoria for the day. He discussed the matter with the authorities and was given permission to bring the group to his home, as long as he agreed to be responsible to guard them and return them to the ship. Dad readily agreed, hung up the phone, and then made some other necessary calls. One was to a friend who had a boat, and the two made arrangements to get the group from the steamer to the shore. The next call was for another driver to join Dad to pick up the people at the dock. The distance was not far, but gas was strictly rationed. With these critical arrangements made, Dad and Mother hurriedly began to prepare more vegetables, get the turkey ready for roasting, and I had to set more tables in the big dining room. Now the guests numbered 41, not 25.

We didn't have many decorations because of the war, but it was still festive. A real Christmas tree stood in a corner of the living room. It exuded the memorable scent of cedar throughout the house. Icicles dripped from the branches reflecting the colored lights, and balls of gold, red, blue, and silver added to the joyous atmosphere of the season.

When the newly-released group walked into our home the next day, the atmosphere was electric. These were missionaries and their children who had paid a heavy price to serve the Lord in China. They had been captured and had spent four years in a prison camp. Some of their group had died from the mistreatment, and the rest were malnourished and so thin that their clothes hung on their bodies. Every eye that welcomed them was wet with tears—tears of realization of the dangers and severe persecution they had suffered at the hands of their captors. Yet here they stood, freed at last and back on their own land. They looked downcast and nervous, as they came into this welcoming group of open arms.

We brought the food in and placed it on the table. The bowls of mashed potatoes, gravy, carrots and green peas gave a vivid color scheme to the table. Then the people were invited to sit down. The children had never seen an orange, a beef roast or a turkey! The adults had not seen such an abundance of food for as long as they could remember. Aromas of beef and turkey filled the house and they reveled in the scents. They sat at the table wide-eyed with awe at the grace of God who had arranged for this time of fellowship with other godly people.

After Dad asked the blessing on the food and the gathering, there was little conversation as the guests filled their plates with satisfying food that pleased both the eye and the palate. It did not take long for the dishes heaped with food to be emptied and filled again. (I remember Dad savoring his portion, the tail of the turkey, with his eyes closed and looking as if it was the best thing he had ever eaten.) When the time for dessert came, Dad, Mother, and I served each person a dish of sliced peaches with a large dollop of real whipped cream. A big plate of dark slices of Christmas cake full of currants, nuts, and candied orange peel with the coffee was a lovely taste treat to end this momentous meal.

Slowly our guests began to talk quietly to others at the tables. When everyone was sated and the conversation began to flow, Dad asked the senior missionary to tell them of their experiences and of the trip across the ocean. The man rose and spoke haltingly of some of their deprivations and the loss of one of the fathers. His descriptions were painful to hear, but they taught us of the price some had paid to tell other nations about Jesus' love and salvation. The missionary recounted the instances of God's faithfulness to them in their dire circumstances and how He upheld them time and time again with His Word and comforting presence.

He then remembered a little book he carried in his pocket, reached in and pulled it out. As he flipped through it, he told of being in Hong Kong the night before they left China. He went to a pagoda on the crest of a hill, where he could look out over the city. His heart was breaking for the people he had learned to love, and he prayed earnestly for the land he had to leave and its unknown future. He said that as he looked around the inside walls of the pagoda, he noticed some English names with Scripture references written underneath them. He read these names aloud.

Suddenly, we heard a gasp. It came from the direction of a couple of the sailors sitting at the table. The two men stood. They said they were the ones who had written their names and those Scripture verses on that very wall in Hong Kong! A stunned silence fell over the room, as we looked at each other with wide-open eyes and big smiles with the "Oh, my!" and "Wow!" being voiced. We could hardly believe what we had heard.

One of the other servicemen took Dad aside and asked if he could take up a collection for these missionaries. "Certainly, go ahead and do it," Dad said. It didn't take long to gather a nice amount of money, which was then handed to the grateful missionary. Word got out to others about this amazing event, and people began to bring gifts and other needed items to the house. One Christian man who owned a shoe store opened it up and fitted every one of them with new shoes.

That eventful day had yet one more emotional moment, for the daughter of one of the missionaries was a nurse in Toronto. Despite the protestations of her parents, Dad decided to make a long-distance call to her. When he made the call, he learned that the daughter was a patient in the hospital where she worked. She had undergone serious brain surgery and was now in recovery. Someone brought a telephone to her room so she and her parents could talk. We could overhear their conversation and tearful sobs, and it affected each one of us deeply. Once more eyes brimmed with unshed tears, but hearts were full of gratitude to God for having a part in such a wonderful day.

At the end of the day, Dad and his friend transported the missionaries back to the dock, where the boat took them back to the rusty steamer. Each one wondered if they would ever meet again this side of heaven. That momentous day was a fitting climax to Dad and Mother's years of ministering to men and women from many walks of life whose lives had been interrupted by war.

Looking back, I am awed how God arranged this healing time for the missionary group. He had the steamer dock at a certain port where there was a man who had the connections to allow them to visit this loving, caring family, who had the house big enough for the entire group to join those already there, and that God had also made sure there was more than enough food for all who were assembled.

Somehow, I think that having at the table the two sailors who wrote their names on the pagoda wall made some special connection with the missionaries and the land they loved. God's tender care in giving them this special loving start to their new life on a New Year's Day was miraculous, and I was privileged to be a part of it. It is still a tender memory for me even to this day.

5

WHEN THERE IS NO INN
FOR THE NIGHT

When World War II ended, Percy Wills returned as a missionary to work with the Shantymen's Christian Association (SCA) in Victoria, although he would be in a more advisory role. It would be quite an adjustment after six years of daily work preparing for the constant coming and going of military service personnel who ate and slept in our home 24/7. It was a rare day when only Percy, Margarette (my father and mother), and I were alone.

Even before we left the big house on Belmont Avenue in Victoria, B.C., my parents were praying and considering what they should do about their housing—what could they do? Rent, or buy? The Lord gave them an answer from friends, who suggested they build a home. Their friends told them there was a nice lot for sale only a few houses away from them, and they offered the use of the blueprints for their home which was a nice floor plan for a two-story, two-bedroom home. Not only that, but a building contractor lived just around the corner from this lot. When Dad contacted him, he agreed to build the house for them. He even finished the attic so we could put extra beds up there for family use. The neighborhood was a quiet one with nicely kept homes and gardens to look at.

We hear the caution, 'Location, location, location.' The site of this lot was exactly what we needed. It was next door to a grocery store, a little fish and chip shop, and a drugstore. A bus stop was at the corner so Mother could take the bus into town when Dad was away with the car. I could ride my bike to the local high school.

With all these things considered, Mom and Dad decided to go ahead and build. When it was completed, we made the move to our new home at the end of the year. My brother Frank was discharged from the Air Force and moved in with us. Once again, our family was together, and a new stage of life began for the four of us.

Percy and Margarette were very hospitable and their home became the hub of many activities related to the mission and their church. They were still in frequent contact with many of the military men and women who had been such a large part of their lives during the war.

Percy was an engaging speaker who loved to tell people what God had done to keep the work on the mission field afloat. From his background of the boat ministry on the west coast of Vancouver Island, B. C., he was frequently asked to talk about that work and how God blessed the missionaries and provided needed funding for the expanded field along the coastline. So many times when the need was made known to the weekly prayer group in Victoria, those faithful ones lifted the request to the Lord and He answered them at the right time so that the funding was more than enough to cover the expenses.

I remember one particular time when Dad was invited to speak at a church about an hour's drive north of Victoria. He invited Mom and me and our friend Julia to go along with him. I was around 17 at the time. It was a cold wintry day late in the Fall. We looked forward to seeing the changing color of the leaves along the route to our destination, as well as the little communities we would pass through.

The route we drove would take us over the Malahat Drive only a few miles north of Victoria. It passed between a forested area and one part where the rocky face of the hill was on the southbound side of the road. The drive over the hill was not that high, but it was fairly steep in places. Otherwise, it was a very scenic part of the trip and we looked forward to traveling it.

When we arrived at the church for the evening meeting it felt good to get out of the cold air outside. We were warmly greeted by the people, many of whom we knew from previous meetings. We had a few minutes to chat with them while Percy and the minister discussed the order of the service.

When it was time for Percy's talk, everyone was eager to hear what he would say. He always spoke of the ways and means that

God used to provide for the work of the mission in the various areas, mentioning specific times God had answered prayers for needed money, supplies, or personnel, sometimes at the last moment. He would credit the work of the other missionaries, but would never say how, or what, he had personally accomplished. His whole aim was to glorify God to those listening.

While Dad was telling a story of God's provision, giving details so people could visualize the incident, his face would reflect the joy he felt in the retelling. His voice would be vibrant, his diction clearly heard, his movements natural and fluid. His whole attitude was full of encouragement that was absorbed by the people listening raptly in the pews (even Mom, Julia and me at that meeting). The whole atmosphere of the church was lifted by the presence of God.

When the service was over, we stayed for a short while for fellowship. However, the evening was getting late and we needed to start the drive back home so we said our good-byes and headed for our car.

Outside of the warmth of the church, the cold air nipped at us and we hastily got in the car hoping the heater would warm up quickly. We also noted that the road had a little sheen of frost on it. But we had to get home and Percy was a careful driver, so we left.

Within the car, we all still felt the presence of the Lord and were full of joy at the way the people at the church had responded to the message Percy gave. Mom, Julia and I talked about what we liked, the questions that came up after the service, and how God was so present. Dad did not talk because he was intent on driving in the dark and cold. After a little while and the car being warm, our talking faded and we began to feel sleepy. We just sat quietly and personally reflected on our own response to the service.

We were approaching the Malahat Drive, noting the trees that were sparkling with the icy frost that covered their leaves and branches. We also saw that the highway that had looked frosty when we left the church now had an icy look to it. But we just expected that we would be able to get home without any problems. We had no sense of trouble, we were just quiet.

The car started up the Malahat hill and we were almost at the top when, suddenly, the motor quit, and we began slowly sliding back down the hill. I don't remember us talking, I think we were stunned at what was happening. I was afraid to look out the back window, in case I saw us sliding off the road. I couldn't see if Dad was moving the steering wheel, or just holding so we slid in a straight line to the bottom of the hilly road.

It was so quiet in the car—dead silence. No one said anything. We were each one absorbed in our own questions. What do we do now? How can we stay warm through the night in the car? How long can we keep the heater going when the motor isn't on? It seemed like a long time, but I guess it was not.

Dad broke the silence, telling us to stay in the car while he approached a few houses across the road that were set back from the highway. There were only four or five, as I remember, and we hadn't seen many houses in that area when we drove by just a few minutes before. The three of us remained silent as our eyes were glued on Dad walking purposefully toward the homes. It was dark, the only light coming from the houses, the moon, and maybe our headlights.

He seemed to know which house to approach because we saw him knock on the door of this one house. The door opened and we saw him talking with the owner of the house. It was just a few minutes later that we saw the door close, and Dad began walking back to us in the car. When he arrived, he told us that we could stay the night at that home.

Still silent, we left the car and followed him to the house, where we were kindly welcomed and the owner showed us to our rooms. Julia and I entered the bedroom we would occupy, and looked at the nicely laid out room with a double bed. We noted how cold the room was, and we learned that it belonged to a daughter of the home who was away at school. It had been closed off and unheated since she left.

Because of the cold, we decided to sleep in our clothes because we were still warm. We quickly pulled back the covers and hoped they were enough to keep us warm during the night. Once we arranged ourselves in the bed and covered up, we lay there not saying much. I guess we were still shaken by the strangeness of this event we were in. We finally warmed up enough to go to sleep until we woke up in the morning.

We were so thankful to the Lord and this family that we could not properly express our feelings. For them to take in four absolute strangers without any kind of fuss was more than we could understand at the time. I'm sure Mom and Dad got their names and made some attempt to show our appreciation for their great kindness to us in our dire situation. Our hearts were flooded with thanksgiving to God for His wonderful provision in such a severe time of need.

We walked back over to the car and noted that the road was not quite as icy. Once seated in the car, we had a prayer time thanking God for what He had just done, and prayed a blessing for the family who were so kind and generous.

Dad turned the key in the ignition and the car started right up. We were no longer quiet, but joyful with praise and thanksgiving. With everything back in the right way, we arrived home not long after with quite a story to tell our loved ones.

As I reflected on this time in my life, it came to me that God was so thoughtful to have Julia with us that night. Had she not been there, I would have had to spend a very cold and lonely night in a strange room. Would I have even been able to warm up without Julia beside me? I had no idea where the room was that my parents occupied. I could not have called out to them. It was a lesson that God lovingly attends to every detail necessary before we even know what the plans are that He is leading us into. Such an event gives me another boost to my faith that God does have my best interests in His heart and will provide in any future trial. All praise and glory be to our majestic Lord Jesus Christ.

6

WHEN YOU'RE UP TO YOUR NECK
IN COLD WATER

In British Columbia, Canada, the West Coast of Vancouver Island is a most beautiful—but rugged—landscape stretching 300 to 400 miles, interspersed with many little inlets, bays, deep water fjords, and larger sounds. The rounded hills and majestic mountains carpeted with the deep green colors of evergreen trees that march down to the water's edge, the grey and brown of the rock outcroppings, contrasted with the deep blue of the ocean, make a feast for the eyes. Native villages are scattered along the coastline in protected areas to keep them from the often lashing waves of the Pacific Ocean.

The Pacific Coast is not only beautiful, it is also most deadly, and rightfully became known as "The Graveyard of the Pacific." Except for the southern tip of Vancouver Island, the rest of the coast has no landmass between it and Japan. Sudden winter storms can build up the power of the winds and waves to such an extent that many a boat is destroyed and many lives lost, never to be found. Fog banks can descend in a short time so the captain of a boat must know the places where he can safely anchor to ride out the storm. Days are shorter in winter and rain is frequent, casting a depressing pall over the atmosphere. Rain can be measured in feet, not in inches.

In the early 1930s, my father, Percy Wills, began a work there under the auspices of the Shantymen's Christian Association (SCA) in a rented fishing boat. The farther he went along the coastline visiting the villages, the more need he found. There was much poverty, both physically and spiritually. They were so isolated, lonely and struggling to survive, but when Percy came to see them, his very presence proved that God had not forgotten them. Percy loved the people and wanted to see them more often, but access to them was limited because there were only logging roads. One either had to go by water, or hike the many trails with a backpack.

It soon became evident that a boat of their own was necessary for the work, but there was no money to buy one. The members of the SCA were men of faith and prayer backed by a weekly prayer meeting in Victoria. They laid the need before the Lord and He answered their prayers with enough money for them to build a boat sturdy and able to take the punishing waves of the Pacific West Coast. In 1934, Messenger II was commissioned. It was an apt name because the boat was taking the Gospel story as a message of God's love to those who had almost no knowledge of Jesus as their Savior.

On his boat visiting the various villages, lumber mills, and isolated people, Percy saw the great need for medical care, added to the other needs for spiritual nurture and human friendship. There was no doctor, no clinic, or hospital where sick or injured people could get help and relief. As was his regular practice, Percy immediately began to pray specifically about this huge need. His complete trust was in God to supply everything—land, building materials, staff and supplies. Later, in 1937, the hospital was built and opened to its first patient. God supplied supernaturally every single thing that was needed. The place was named "Esperanza," which means "Hope." It truly was a place of hope, as well as healing. Every patient was prayed for and told of Jesus' sacrifice on the cross for the forgiveness of their sins. And their physical needs were tended with love and great care.

Meanwhile, there was a doctor with a medical practice in Bella Coola, B.C., who had been asking the Lord to send him to the "hardest place on the West Coast." News travels fast in those regions, and Percy soon heard of Herman Alexander McLean, contacted him, and invited him to join him on a voyage for a week. Percy knew where the "hardest place on the West Coast" was. That time with Percy was an eye-opener for the doctor, and he realized that God was directing him to join him in his work.

Once Dr. McLean, referred to as "Doc," joined Percy in the mission work, Doc's wife Marion and their five children moved to Esperanza and became a major part of the work there. With the hospital as a base, Doc traveled in the Messenger II up and down the coastline to other locations attending to patients who did not need the hospital services.

In September of 1948, Doc, Marion, and their two older children, Don and Shirley, were visiting at Chamis Bay for a few days to hold services and visit the sick. They intended to return home at the end of their trip. However, a storm blew in that made it too difficult for sea travel. Air travel was now available, so his wife and daughter flew home, leaving Doc and Don with the boat.

For several days, the storm continued unabated. Doc had felt a deep unease about this trip but did not want to mention it to anyone. He and Don tried to get closer to home but the attempt was blocked when the water pump quit and they were forced to let the wind drive them until they could get back to safety. Doc's uneasiness increased and he became afraid that this trip would end in some kind of danger. He decided to put the boat into the care of a friend at Chamis Bay and he and Don flew home. When the plane touched down at the hospital dock, Doc's relief was great and their loved ones welcomed them with loving arms.

After many days the winter weather finally improved and Doc decided to fly back to Chamis Bay to retrieve the repaired boat which was so necessary at the hospital. His 15 year-old son, Bruce, dearly wanted to go with him but Doc's deep unease still troubled him. Though he was familiar with travel between various villages lining the inland waterways, he was not a real expert seaman on the Pacific Ocean. He trembled just thinking about retrieving the boat and the possibility of sudden storms. Storms on the Pacific Coast in winter could be very strong and 30-foot waves were not uncommon. Even large ships were destroyed on the rocky coast. He tried to dissuade Bruce, but his son was insistent that he accompany his dad so Doc bought two tickets for the plane ride back to Chamis Bay.

Bruce was so happy to be with his dad, but Doc was even more uneasy, although he would not say anything about it. Though he was apprehensive, he was glad to have Bruce's company. They boarded the boat, Doc started the engine, and they began the several hours trip to Esperanza.

All seemed to go well until the winds began howling and water started pouring in to the pilot house with every wave. Bruce became very seasick and lay on his bunk. Meanwhile, Doc was trying desperately to keep the boat from turning over. He asked Bruce to check the bilge to see if there was water in it. The boat was pitching so violently that Bruce could hardly stand up. It worsened his misery, but he managed to get down to the engine room only to find water sloshing around everywhere. Even the wiring for the engine was soaked. Bruce tried to put more gas in the fuel pump, but that was almost impossible to do. He went back to report what he found.

They were only about 15 minutes from home when suddenly the engine sputtered and quit. Doc frantically tried to get it to restart. It would not. When he tried to pump the bilge, the pump broke. With the wet wiring, the controls could be affected in handling the boat. Everything seemed to be against them. The winds and the waves were tossing the boat around so badly they knew they were in danger of being blown onto the rocks nearby. They had tried every possible thing they knew to do. There was nothing more that could be done. They had to abandon ship. A sense of hopelessness came upon them. Each of them tried to envision what that would be like. Where on the coastline were they? Maybe in the skiff they could find a small cove where they could weather the storm until it broke.

Doc went out on the heaving deck to try to get the skiff ready but a sudden burst of wind took an oar. That hope was dashed. Holding tightly to the rope railing and trying to keep his footing, he tried to drop an anchor, hoping it would grab on the bottom and keep the ship steady. It did go overboard and, for a minute or two, it seemed to hold, but even that did not work. The boat was still moving toward the reefs. Doc went back inside and told Bruce that prayer was now their only recourse.

They prayed that God would have His perfect will. They were not afraid to die, but they greatly feared the raging waters and the whirling winds dashing the boat against the rocks. Doc put a lifebelt on Bruce and one on himself. Then having done all that they could possibly do, they laid on their bunks praying, awaiting the inevitable.

When they felt the impact they knew the time had come. There was no light, so they groped their way to the deck on the side away from the rocks, feeling their way to the back of the boat. Just then, a monstrous breaker hit the side of the boat hurling it into the air. Both of them tumbled into the water between the boat and the rocks. They were separated, never to see each other again this side of Heaven.

Doc began desperately swimming trying to reach some type of land. He was gasping for air in the icy wind and water. The breakers were still crashing against the reefs, and the need for air was quickly draining his strength. As he was about to take his last breath, he hit the bottom of the boat. Just then, God lifted him above the waves. Doc took another breath and fell back into the tumultuous water.

Now he was at the mercy of the waves and again in danger of drowning. Just then, another wave washed over him and left him on a rock. He clung to the rock with desperate, clawing fingers. Another wave hit. As it receded, he climbed higher and clung on tightly as yet another wave crashed over him, almost sweeping him off his temporary perch. God became his strength to hold on, and to climb higher when the waves receded. He was able to get to the pinnacle of his rock of refuge where he held on for dear life, being battered by the waves about every five minutes. It was a place of safety and he thanked God for being alive. He did not know if he would live or die there on that rock but he again committed his life to his Lord Jesus.

What is he thinking now that he is "safe"? It must be around midnight—about 12 hours since he and Bruce left Chamis Bay and the real world. There is no light of any kind. He cannot see anything, even the rock he is on. He is shivering in the cold. He is wet to the bone and cannot get dry or warm. The tide is getting lower but the storm is still strong. The noise of winds, the water crashing against the reefs are the only sounds he hears. Adding to this misery is his grief in the realization that his son is dead and his body will never be found. If he himself dies there, will his body be found? Will his boat be shredded to pieces by the force of the water against it? No other ships are out in this storm, and if there were, they could not see him in the blackness of night. He must have felt like a blip in the dark.

Amid all these considerations Doc's prayers rose to God about the remains of the boat. He asked that the boat be near so that when daylight comes and the tide is out, he could reach it to possibly get some dry clothing, some food to eat, and rope to tie himself to this rock. He did not know how long he would be there, or how long the storm would last. His only hope was God's mercy to keep him alive. He thought of his family, his dear wife, who was such a brave and godly partner with him in his work. He thought of his children as they were reaching adulthood, how would God lead them into His plans for their lives? His patients—how were they doing in recovery? Slowly the night passed and the first glimmers of daylight began to show. It seemed as if the waves were not as high, the tide had turned, the wind was not as strong. Now he could see some shapes in his surroundings. Rocks, more rocks, but there, not far away, was his boat. Relief flooded his body! God had not forgotten him. He had heard his cries.

The boat was impaled on the rocks nearby so that he could get on it to gather what he needed to survive. As he looked at it, he could read its name, Messenger II. It was his message from God that he was not alone. It was almost like having a friend at his side. He was no longer a blip in the dark. There was wreckage for a passing ship to see. Hope began to rise in his soul.

From his vantage point on the rock, Doc could see the vast expanse of ocean. Nothing blocked his view. His rock of refuge had become his periscope to rescue. Had the boat crashed farther into the bay he would not have this wide view of the waters. His vista would have been limited.

As soon as the waters got low enough, Doc left his place and managed to get across the reefs to the boat, gathered the things he needed, and made it back to his rock. He began to scan the horizon for any sign of shipping but nothing was in view. The day slowly went by, the storm abated more. In preparation for the night he tied himself to the rock so he could not be washed off. He spent the second night in the same situation—total darkness, high tide and constant waves keeping him wet. There was no chance to sleep.

The next morning, Doc continued to search the horizon, hoping and praying that God would send help very soon. A little later, he strained to see if what he thought he saw was real. Was that smoke on the horizon? A ship? Could it be a ship? How he hoped against hope that his eyes were not deceiving him. Hardly daring to breathe, Doc watched as it became more and more certain that it was a ship.

Madly, Doc grasped a sheet and started waving it wildly in the clear air, praying that here was his chance of life again. His eyes were glued on the ship. Did it see him? Which way was it going? Is it turning? The ship began to turn in his direction. His rescuer was coming!

It was a trolling vessel of the Kyuquot Trollers Association heading back to its port. It altered its course and anchored as close as it could get. He saw a skiff being lowered and men in it headed directly for him. He could hardly wait for them to get past the reefs and take him into the vessel. He knew that he was now safe.

Once he was on board the troller, Doc collapsed on the deck. Deep, groaning, wracking sobs welled up from his innermost being. The realization that he would live was almost more than he could handle. He almost felt reborn, knowing that God still had a purpose for him.

On the same night that Doc was clinging to his rock of refuge, Mother and I were at a meeting in Victoria. Suddenly an usher came and quietly told us that word had come from the hospital at Esperanza that Doc and Bruce were missing. He also said no word had come from my father and his shipmate, Harold Peters, who were on the boat, Messenger III. We immediately left for home, greatly troubled in heart and mind.

Now we, too, were involved in this drastic situation. Where were Dad and Harold? What has happened to them? Are they adrift at sea, too? Our hearts were heavy with fear for their safety. (When one of the family is in a dangerous occupation, such as law enforcement under cover work, there always seems to be that thread of fear residing in the back of the mind). We tried to think of someone to call for information, but nobody knew anything. We spent a troubled night. Lots of questions, but no answers were forthcoming.

The next day we got news that Dad and Harold were safe. They had found a cove where they anchored during the storm, but there was no radio service to let anyone know where they were until they could leave their place of safety. Once they were back at sea they heard the S.O.S. about Doc and Bruce, and headed straight for Esperanza to be with the grieving family and others at the mission base. They did not know anything about Doc's travail except that he could not be reached to find out why he and Bruce had not returned. Once Doc was back at Esperanza, he told everyone what had happened, and that Bruce had drowned.

After such a harrowing time, Doc could have decided it was just too dangerous there and taken his family inland to a safer place to minister to the needs of the people. But that was not his heart. In his deep concern for the welfare of his patients, Doc was soon back to work visiting the various places where his healing arts were needed. He continued to travel up and down the West Coast for many more years.

As I wrote this story I began to wonder, Who among us has not had a major storm—or two or three—take us by surprise? Storms that turn our life on end, storms that seem to last forever? We wonder—will we ever get out of it? How will we get through it with some sanity left? The current situation in our country has given thousands of people a very huge storm in the last two or three years.

Often, that is when God becomes our "rock of refuge," our Guide to the way out of it, the One Who keeps us sane when everything looks scrambled. He has promised that He will never leave or forsake us…ever! He is God of the present, and he knows the beginning up until the ending of our days here on earth. He has no limits of any kind and can bring our lives back into order out of the chaos of the storms.

7

When God Is Your Mechanic

When World War II ended in 1945, everything began to open up. Here in Canada, the servicemen and women were demobilized and ready to come back home and start a new life in a renewed economy. People were thrilled to have their loved ones back home again. Rationing was out and you could buy all the food you wanted. Women's skirt levels dropped to mid-calf because more cloth was available for sewing. Former service-men were now out of uniform and could buy new clothing for their wardrobes. Families started taking road trips now that gas was readily available and the speed limit was raised.

Nylon was a new synthetic material developed by DuPont Company in 1935. I read that it was named "Nylon" for the two cities, New York and London, where the research was done. It became very useful during the War for parachutes and airplane cord and ropes. After the war, it became useful for consumers. The word "Nylon" became familiar for women's stockings rather than silk.

More housing was needed for the returned veterans, and because of the demand for wood, metals and such, all contracts were written as Cost Plus. One could sign a contract for a certain amount, but the final cost price was usually more as prices for commodities kept rising to meet the demand.

Around that time builders began building large tracts of houses with different floor plans instead of one at a time. A finished house of each floor plan was opened for public viewing so a potential buyer could choose the one best suited to their desires. Mortgages could be arranged for financing the house with payments over time at a certain percentage. Sales were up as the returning veterans, many newly married, wanted to own their own homes.

One group who also was eager to return to their fields of labor were the missionaries who had to leave their stations during the war. Many arranged to get back to the people they loved and share the Gospel with them once more. They wondered if the Christians had grown in their faith and were telling others what God had done for them.

My father, Percy Wills, was one of the missionaries with Shantymen's Christian Association (SCA). Soon he was back on a boat visiting the people on the West Coast of Vancouver Island. The visits were very meaningful both to Percy and the people in the villages and lighthouses, who had not had much spiritual guidance and comfort during the years of the war. Long-time friendships and new believers were so glad to see each other and catch up on the news that happened during that time.

It soon became evident that what SCA had was inadequate to meet the growing needs of the coastal people. The board of directors for the Mission decided to build a new, and larger 50-foot boat to be named Messenger III. God provided a man, Harold Peters, who was a seasoned mariner to pilot that larger ship.

Percy and Harold served in Messenger III until a doctor told him he could not continue to do the strenuous boat work. He then moved his ministry back to land to continue in a more administrative role in Victoria, B. C. In 1948 he met a couple in Seattle, Washington, who dreamed of using a post-war naval vessel as a floating hospital. The husband, Captain C. F. Stabbert, was in the construction business but felt God calling him into missionary service. Their meeting was designed by the Lord and the two men became fast friends. As their friendship grew, "Cap" Stabbert told Percy of his desire. He purchased a naval minesweeper from the United States government and began to refit it as a hospital ship. He incorporated the mission under the name Marine Medical Mission. Plans went ahead and the ship was soon set to make its maiden voyage in July 1949, with Percy on board.

When the Messenger III was completed in 1949, she was docked at the wharf in the beautiful Inner Harbor in Victoria, where there was a very special and unusual dedication service scheduled to take place. A couple of unidentified newspaper clippings tell about the event, one of which, dated Friday, July 22, 1949, read as follows:

"A dedication service for three medical-mission boats—two Canadian and one American—will be held in the Inner Harbor in front of the Parliament Buildings Sunday evening. "The service is unique in that it is seldom that crafts engaged in this work are in the same locality at one time.

"The three boats are the 135-foot Willis Shank, converted U.S. Navy minesweeper of the Marine Medical Mission, Seattle; the Bruce McLean, speedy new craft of the Nootka Hospital (later Esperanza General Hospital), and the Messenger III of the SCA.

"There are stories behind the names of two of the ships. The Willis Shank is named after a Seattle Youth for Christ leader who was killed in a plane crash while flying to Alaska to dedicate a new mission, and the Bruce McLean is named for the fifteen-year-old son of Dr. H. A. McLean, who was drowned when the Messenger II was wrecked on the reefs near Tatchu Point on the west coast of the island on Oct. 2, last year."

One of the news items noted that about 1,500 people lined the embankment by the Parliament Buildings to watch the proceedings. The three skippers were Captain C. Stabbert of the Willis Shank, Harold Peters of the Messenger III, and Percy Wills, looking after the Bruce McLean at that time. The article stated that the Willis Shank was en route to Alaska to visit the sparsely populated islets off the coast of British Columbia and Alaska to provide medical and spiritual help to the indigenous people at its ports of call.

According to their website, whenever the Willis Shank arrived at a new port, the crew would blare Christian music from a bullhorn speaker up on the mast. When people heard the music, they would gather at the dock to welcome the ship. While the ship was docked, one team would attend to the medical cases, one team would hold meetings to preach the gospel, and, in the summer, Bible College students would volunteer to hold Bible study classes for the children.

Later, Percy told me this story. One day, the Willis Shank approached Bella Coola, B.C., intending to hold some children's meetings there. Bella Coola is a fishing port at the mouth of the Bella Coola river. It is also the heart of the Great Bear Rain Forest and Chilcotin Plateau and the First Nations culture. It sits in a ring of majestic snow-clad mountains, lovely with green grass, and the dark green forests surrounded by the deep blue sky. It is now the administrative center for the B.C. central coast.

As a ship of American registry, Capt. Stabbert had to request permission from the Canadian authorities to put in at that port. Permission was denied. I have wondered why, and there is no one who can tell me. I surmised that it might be the length and size of the ship, 135-feet, in comparison to the size of the port. I don't know if the fishing boats, or wharfs, at that time were big enough to accommodate such a large vessel.

After permission was denied, the ship started to sail toward Alaska, but the engine soon began to experience problems and make really unusual, clanking noises. All went quiet in the wheelhouse. What on earth could be wrong? We've never heard that kind of sound before. The ship was thoroughly retrofitted only a few years ago, at most. Quickly, the captain scanned all the meters in front of him but none of them seemed to be out of order. He immediately cut the speed and began turning the ship around while others began to pray for God's help in finding out what went wrong.

Since the ship had not gone far from Bella Coola, Capt. Stabbert radioed for permission to pull into port there in an emergency. This time permission was granted and the ship tied up at the wharf.

Now that they would be docked for several days while the mechanics were tearing down the large engine, the rest of the staff decided to see if they could hold some Bible classes for the children. They spread out in the town and visited some of the homes, inviting the people to an impromptu Bible study. The medical team opened the boat to those who were in need of their help.

After tearing the huge engine down and checking several possibilities, they finally found the cause. A bolt had come loose and gone through the reduction gear. (A reduction gear is one small gear, driven by the engine. It drives a large gear which is connected to the propeller shaft.) The gear was not damaged, but the teeth of the gear had crimped the bolt! Who ever heard of such a thing? It was not possible for that to happen. The stunned engine mechanic yelled, "Hey Guys, come over here and see this thing! You won't believe your eyes!" It was such a wonder that even those who didn't know anything about mechanics could see that God had indeed worked a miracle to get the Willis Shank into that port. He made a way for them to tell the children and adults the old, old story of Jesus and His love.

I have no explanation as to why God chose Bella Coola to work this miracle and there is no one alive who can tell me. Maybe there was one soul who needed to hear the Gospel message of salvation, or maybe someone on the crew needed to see a miracle to strengthen their faith. Perhaps they had prayed together and discerned the Lord's will for them to go to that port, and they needed to see how God would make a way where there seemed to be no way. My father witnessed many of the same kinds of miracles in his long years of service, and he made sure I knew about the small crimped bolt that made it necessary for the ship to be docked in the place the Lord had chosen to bring His loving care. God can open a door no one can shut. He does it all the time. It's His specialty.

8

WHEN EVERYONE'S IN THE RIGHT PLACE AT THE RIGHT TIME

This story would have a vastly different outcome if there had not been the specific right persons present at the time of the event, the specific right places at the specific right times of need. Only by the masterful arrangement of our wise and loving Lord Jesus does this story work out for the best possible ending.

School was out for the summer. My three sons, Stephen, Dale, and John were enjoying the long days free of homework and classes. My husband Bob pastored a small church in a neighboring town a few miles away. His parents, Michael and Amanda, and Grandma Barr, Amanda's mother, lived next door to us in a quiet middle-class neighborhood in San Gabriel Valley, California. We were a close-knit, happy family. Our neighbors were friendly and our boys played with their children. Life was good.

I worked full time as cashier at the local J. C. Penney store, and Bob was frequently gone on church business during the day. For us, weekends were spent getting ready for the church services on Sunday. Intermingled in this schedule were Little League baseball practices, music lessons, baseball games, and after school events.

As with most churches in those days, Wednesday nights were set for prayer meetings when people would gather to pray for their people of interest, or the current needs of the country, and other matters pertinent to each church. And so it was with our church. Bob and I were usually there on Wednesday nights. Ordinarily, Bob's mother Amanda or another older lady friend would stay with our boys while we were gone. But for whatever reason on this Wednesday night in late June of 1965, Bob decided to stay at home while I attended the meeting. I think that was the only time in several years that he did not go to the church.

After supper, I left for the meeting. Bob began to work on something in the garage. Dale, who was twelve, and John, who was ten, went outside to play with some friends.

Steve, who was fourteen at the time, was in the house. This is what he recalled: "I was at home in the living room, probably reading or watching TV. I heard a horrendous noise at the porch. I really thought the kids were screaming and making as much noise as possible just for fun and to be obnoxious. I opened the door and made some remark to get them to shut up and stop pretending. I recall Dale saying, 'No, Steve! Look at the porch!' I looked down and it was covered in blood."

John explained to me what happened. "We were playing around near a telephone pole and I saw a temporary spike step on the lower portion of the pole. As a 10-year-old, I'm not sure how high that first spike was but it might have been about 5-6 feet off of the ground. I wondered if I could climb that pole just for the fun of it. I don't recall if I was able to get up on that first spike on my own, or if one of my friends or my brother lifted me up and on it. I remember standing on the spike on my left foot and clutching the next highest spike with my left hand. I looked up and to the right to see the next permanent spike on the pole. I thought if I could jump up and reach it, I would then be able to climb that pole as high up as I wanted to. I remember looking up and planning my next move. I jumped and my right hand missed the spike. I tried to push myself away from the pole as I dropped, when suddenly I felt something in my right arm pit. It was an intense pressure but without initial pain. I remember telling my brother Dale, 'I think it's in me!' I reached over with my left hand to feel the spike. It was well within my armpit. As I pulled my hand away I saw blood and knew I was hurt. I was now hanging off of the ground by the spike inside my armpit. Since my feet were still off the ground, I think it was my brother Dale who lifted me off the pole. Screaming loudly, he ran across the street and home to get help.

"My father came to the door and told me to stay on the porch. I think he told my eldest brother Steve to go get some towels. My father wrapped a towel tightly around my chest and drove to a medical clinic on Peck Road, one that I had seen while driving by many, many times on our way to and from church. I can still picture that building in my mind."

My son Steve stayed at the house. He said after they left, he got a hose and hosed off the porch. It was just as traumatic for him. He said, "In those days before cell phones, once they'd left the house there was no way to make contact to find out what was going on. So I was in shock and suspense maybe a little panicky until one of my parents called or came home with some news."

That must have been a very traumatic time for Steve to be alone. The rest of us were totally caught up in John's care, so he had to bear his fears alone until he learned the outcome of the surgery. (Looking back later on, I wondered if I even thanked Steve and Dale for their heroic efforts of that night. Since I went from the church directly to the clinic, I did not have any part in the turmoil and chaos all the others went through).

Dale went with Bob to the medical clinic to keep pressure on the towel covering the wound. He was able to stay calm during the ride, which is a great ability he has when a crisis comes up, and a great aid to his father who was also trying to stay calm. God was with them in the car.

While this was going on at home, I was at the meeting. About a half hour into it, one of the men had a telephone call. Bob told him what had happened and that I needed to meet them at the Industrial Emergency Clinic about a mile from our home. I asked that man to close up the church, and I ran to my car.

My heart was in my mouth. I was shaking and fearful, trying not to cry as I thought over what I just heard. I tried to focus on driving as quickly as I could to get to the clinic. When I arrived there, I ran in and saw the doctor who briefed me on John's injury. He told me my son would have to go immediately to the hospital for surgery. He had bandaged John's wound and called for the ambulance. When the ambulance came, I climbed in beside John. I was still shocked and shaken, and feeling really cold inside during that ride.

I remember how loud the siren was during the long drive to the hospital where the doctor had privilege. It was in a neighboring town several miles away from our town. Actually, any hospital was quite a few miles from our town, so we were very thankful to God that the clinic was available to us in this emergency.

John said, "I can recall being secured in the back of the ambulance with my mother beside me. As one of the attendants began to close the back door, I can vividly recall seeing my brother Dale and my father standing behind the ambulance and Dale was crying."

Bob and Dale went back home to Steve to tell him the news about John. Then Bob left Steve and Dale together at home and drove to the hospital. They probably went next door to be with their grandparents and alert them to what had just taken place. Meanwhile, I was in the ambulance with John, and the doctor was on his way to prepare for the surgery.

"It was getting dark outside by then and things had happened very quickly," John said. "I knew I was hurt badly and I was very scared. The next thing I remember was waking up in a strange place. I was told I was in a hospital and that I had surgery to fix my arm. Unlike the initial injury, now I could feel intense pain on the right side of my upper chest and it hurt to move. Even if I moved my foot, pain consumed all of the upper right side of my body. I believe I received somewhere in the area of 25-30 stitches in my armpit."

Bob met me at the hospital and we sat in the waiting room praying with anguished prayers for the surgery to be successful. After some time, the surgeon came out to tell us what the injury was. John had cut his right axillary vein, and had lost a lot of blood. The ends of the vein had retracted so that he could not suture them back together. He had to tie each end off which meant that the other smaller veins would have to take on the larger flow of blood down his arm. He warned us that John could possibly have a permanently swollen arm due to the extra pressure on the smaller veins. He also said that he saw the nerve very close to the cut and, hopefully, it would not be affected. It turned out that doctor had just finished a course at UCLA hospital in vein surgery and repair.

The doctor said he thought John's blood level could be brought back by natural means without needing a blood transfusion, but they would do that if it was deemed necessary while he was recuperating. A friend donated a pint of blood for John.

Very mixed emotions took over our minds and conversation on the way home. It ranged back and forth between thanking and praising God's mighty hand in giving us this surgeon with his specific knowledge of treating the injury, and the deeply felt questions about how John's future would be affected.

When we got back home we told everyone what the surgeon did and what John's prognosis for the future was. Again, we were all grateful to the Lord that John's arm was whole and the blood flow was restored, even if it was not the normal way. Before I could go to bed, I had to wash John's clothing. I put them in the washing machine and turned it on. Almost immediately the water started turning very red from the blood. It was so hard to see how much blood was on his clothing. I had to let the washer fill up, then drain it, then fill it again in order to wash his clothing in fresh, clear, soapy water.

After five days, John was able to come home. I went back to work, Bob continued his ministry. And though John couldn't go out for a while, Steve and Dale were back to enjoying their summer days off from school.

While John's arm was still in a sling, July 4th came about. Bob hadn't bought any fireworks but Steve, who was interested in chemistry, had made a few. Among our friends was a family with three children, and their son could make firecrackers. They invited us to come over and enjoy the evening with them. It was a pleasant time sharing our fireworks and getting back into visiting among friends. However, I found that my nerves were still fairly raw. With each "bang" of the firecrackers, I jumped. I was glad to get home to stillness and quiet. It was months before I could hear a siren, or children screaming, and not grow cold and shaky, even though I knew that God had healed John and he was back playing, running, and having fun.

John said, "The pain began to slowly dissipate over time but not soon enough for me. I remember that as a result of the injury to my right arm, I wasn't able to play in the Little League All-Star game that year, a big deal to a 10 year old kid who loved baseball then, and now!

"But I finally reached full recovery. Other than a nasty scar in my right arm pit, after 56 years I still have absolutely no long-term effects of that severe injury to my arm. I was able to continue my enjoyment of competitive sports through high school and beyond without any complication. I still enjoy playing sports with my grandchildren, now inhibited only by my age.

"I was also able to enjoy full employment and a successful career in a field where full use of my arm was a necessary component.

"The exact length of time it took to come back to full use of my arm I'm not sure, but what I am sure about is that it was truly a miracle that I lived and fully recovered. It's more of a miracle looking back at the circumstances knowing what I know now at my age.

"At the tender age of 10, could I understand that I eluded death and that my ultimate full recovery was a miracle? As a child it would be very difficult to fully comprehend the extent of my injury, the potential for losing too much blood too quickly, any complication during a new and complex surgery, or the fragility of life. But prayers were answered and spiritual intervention orchestrated the outcome so I could tell of my experience to encourage others.

"There is no question in my mind that it was God who scheduled my father to be home on that particular Wednesday night, and it was God who scheduled a surgeon recently trained in the subject of my specific injury to be on duty on that particular Wednesday night.

"For those first 10 years of my life I had grown up in the church. I was in Sunday school every week. I had been in and around the church more in those few years than most people twice my age. I don't specifically recall having that personal interaction with God during the time of my injury and recovery, but I do remember being told people were praying for me. And as I sit and write this story today, looking back, there is no doubt in my mind that my Father in Heaven, my personal Savior surely answered those prayers."

So much of John's healing and recovery depended on explicit details of who was where and when. Had John's father not stayed home, his mother could not have handled the situation and John would have perished. If Steve and Dale were not there, each in his own place, the other kids would have freaked out. They were real first responders—heroes. If there had not been a medical clinic a mile from our home, John would have died on the way to a hospital. If another doctor had to do that delicate surgery, John's future, if he survived, would have been quite different.

Even after all this time, when watching John playing with his grandchildren, at times I marvel at the foresight of God. Only He, Who sees the end from the beginning and everything in between, knew this accident would happen and had orchestrated all things necessary down to the last and finest detail. How great is our God, and how worthy of our trust in Him for every moment that we live.

9

WHEN DEATH STARES YOU IN THE FACE

It was a lovely sunny Saturday morning. I had recently retired and was enjoying my freedom. It looked like a nice day for my husband and me to do something interesting. Breakfast was over and we were beginning to start the day when the telephone rang.

It was my son, Dale. He said, "Mom, Jason's been in an accident and we are at the hospital in Riverside. Will you call Elizabeth and pick her up and bring her to the hospital?" His voice was calm with no hint of the dire news we would soon hear. I was in shock. My thirteen-year-old grandson was in the hospital. I wanted to know why, but his father had not given me any more information, only that he had been in an accident.

I immediately phoned Jason's mom and arranged to pick her up at their home not far away. Elizabeth and I were both anxious and silent as we headed to the hospital to find out what had happened.

When we walked into the waiting room, we were surprised to see the large number of people already gathered on our behalf. Elizabeth's parents had arrived, and we joined their pastor and a number of their church friends who had come to back our family in prayer. I knew the pastor had three services the next morning and it touched my heart that he and his group had taken this time to minister to us. How grateful we were for their support in this time of uncertainty!

We were told that Jason's injuries were life-threatening and he was already in the operating room. In the ambulance, his heart had stopped a couple of times and had to be restarted. During the operation, they had to start it a few more times. According to the doctors, Jason's injuries were severe and the outlook bleak.

We found out later that Jason's friend Ryan had invited him to go to his sister's softball game, but when Ryan's father picked him up in his El Camino, which is like a pickup with the back flatbed part open, the others were already packed in the cab, so Jason was told to sit in the back. Minutes later, as they were pulling out of a 4-way stop in the middle of the downtown area, a station wagon that some kid had stolen barreled into the side of the El Camino, the impact hurling Jason 32 feet. He landed hard on his head on the pavement. The ambulance was there almost instantly. Medics determined that Jason's life was in danger so he was rushed immediately to the hospital, where it was found that he sustained three brain hematomas. This meant that there was significant bleeding on the brain. His brain swelled so badly from the impact that the doctors had to drill a golf ball-sized hole in each side of his skull to relieve the pressure. He had also fractured his right wrist and left ankle, and his right ankle had a compound fracture. The brain swelling was so severe they were going to have to put him into a chemically induced coma.

We were all so troubled by this report that fear for Jason's future gripped our hearts and minds. It was very sobering, realizing how much we needed God's intervention to save Jason's life. Our prayers were deep, heartfelt, and emotional. It was almost like there were no words adequate to express the need. We knew God was his only hope.

Meanwhile, Dale was in the hospital room with his son. The doctors were trying to give Jason the medicine to put him in a coma, but he was fighting them, so Dale stood at his bedside and placed his hand on his son's stomach "to give him a human transfusion from his own energy. While he was there the nursing shift change came and Dale started to leave, but they asked him to stay because when he was touching his son, Jason quit fighting them against the injection.

Several hours later, the surgeons came to us to give their report. They were cautiously hopeful that he would make it through the night. He was in a coma and placed in the Children's ICU and given medication to decrease the swelling in his brain. Until his brain stopped swelling none of his broken bones could be reset. And there was another problem. There was only a small window of time to set the bones before they might have to amputate his right foot. The doctors said that Jason had a 3% chance to live, 2% to come back in a vegetative state, and 1% to remain normal.

Later that afternoon we all dispersed with loving hugs and thank you's heartfully given to all those of the church who had stayed and buoyed us up with their presence and prayers through the long hours. Our family stayed to talk about the situation. Norma, Jason's other grandmother, told us that while she was waiting, she saw an angel, and so felt that Jason would pull through. It was a bright note in an otherwise awful day.

Thus began daily trips to the hospital. One of Elizabeth's family brought their motor home so that we all could sit there while we waited for a turn to visit Jason. We were allowed to see him in ICU, one at a time for a few minutes. The nurses and doctors were very kind and would answer our questions as best they could. When it was my turn to spend time with my grandson, I would brush his forehead with my hand and softly sing to him, hoping he could hear me and know he was loved and prayed for. It was strange to see him lying there inert when he was usually so active.

Jason's injuries were so severe and his chances so slim that we could have despaired, but God had more support already in place for this young man's healing. We learned that Riverside General Hospital had the best Head Trauma Unit in that whole area. Also, "it just happened" that his head surgeon was the Chief of the Neurology Department at University Hospital in Loma Linda, nearby. These pieces of information were such a help in keeping our faith up in God's awareness of the need and His careful provision of optimum human help for the sake of Jason's survival and recovery.

Eventually the swelling in Jason's head went down and the doctors were able to set his bones. When those surgeries were completed, both of Jason's ankles and his arm were encased in casts. At one point, the only place they could insert a needle for an injection was his big toe. Later, the holes in Jason's skull were sealed up with 22 surgical grade staples on each side. Jason was in the coma for eleven days until at last he opened his eyes.

Recently I asked Jason what he recalled of that time. This is what he told me. "I don't remember the exact moment I woke up from the coma. I do remember one night being awake, but in a dark quiet room. I wasn't sure where I was. I stared at the white casts on both legs and my right forearm. It just didn't make sense. What happened? Who did this? I thought someone had put long socks on both legs, and a matching one on my right forearm. What I didn't realize is that my right wrist and both ankles were fractured… I wasn't sure where I was, so I climbed out of bed and stood up on my casts to explore. I quickly realized that the bottom of my casts were very difficult to walk on. I remember falling hard on the floor and I couldn't get up. I found out later that I was also connected to an IV delivering pain-relieving morphine. The nurses were pretty mad about the fall.

"Days later, I remember feeling happy and being escorted outside in a wheel chair to join family in a grassy park area. We congregated around a park bench under the sun. As I looked around, I saw my reflection in a nearby window. My head was shaved and I saw shiny zippers on both sides above my ears. When I asked what they were, someone told me I had 44 staples in my head, 22 on each side. Apparently, the impact of being ejected from the El Camino and landing on my head was so bad, it made my head swell like a fully inflated balloon."

Jason continued slowly improving, and after a few weeks, he was transferred to another hospital where he received various therapies to enable him to walk, to recover his speech and to understand what he heard or read.

During this time we celebrated his 14th birthday with a party. Many cards and notes came from teachers and fellow students at his junior high school.

Jason progressed in his rehab quickly in this new facility so that he was discharged a few weeks later. What a wonderful day that was! We were rejoicing in the great goodness of our Lord Jesus, who had brought Jason out of near darkness into His glorious light of life.

Finally Jason was home, and would have normally entered Corona High School but that was impossible for him. Corona High School had a large student body and a large campus. Jason was still recuperating and it would be awhile before he could walk easily, or carry a backpack, or be one of hundreds of students hurrying in the halls to get to the next class.

Jason's other grandparents lived in a quiet little town in Northern California and they offered to take him to live with them there. It was a less stressful area and would aid in his recovery. Dale would not leave his son, so he left everything to Elizabeth and moved with Jason to Northern California. He was determined to do everything he could to help Jason adjust to the new surroundings and do the things needed to fully recover. It wasn't a sudden restoration. Jason required continuing therapies. He had to work hard to regain physical balance and stamina. Dale was devoted to his son, and the effort required for Jason's total recovery was a blessing of bonding for them both.

I followed Jason's progress with great interest and a lot of prayer. He was able to keep up with his school work and graduated with his class of sixty students.

Looking back over the years, I remember praying by Jason's bedside as he lay motionless in a coma, his head swollen, casts on his limbs. What would he be like when he awoke—if he ever woke up? The doctors had said there was only a 1% chance he would have a normal life. Now Jason is one of the top ten people in his field, and, a few years ago, was actually able to run in a marathon.

Recently I asked Jason how the accident affected him. This is what he told me.

"After the accident, I felt so small, but God's plan seemed so big! His presence in my life shifted from seeming like an absent relative to my ever-present Heavenly Father who wanted to be intimately involved in every little detail. I stopped counting my shortfalls, and stayed focused on His will for me. What was His unique strategy in each situation, and how did he want me to do it? Suddenly, I jumped from part-time jobs to being deeply rooted in a full-time fundraising opportunity for a major Idaho-based ministry. But this career path took discipline and obedience I didn't naturally have, so I prayed and asked God for it. Now, each morning my wife and I pray, and then we read our Bible together. And wow, He's continued to pour out His blessings! Praise Him from whom all blessings flow! Like a lamp plugged into the wall, I stay plugged into Jesus as my source of everything.

"Additionally, the Lord has continued to surround me with wise Christian leaders who have taught me how to pray with a confidence in Who he is, and what He can do. I've learned that nothing is impossible with Him, and He supplies the fruit of my labor."

It has been such a pleasure to follow Jason's life with all its ups and downs through the years and to pray for, and with, him as he grew into adulthood. To know this man of God who has been trained by Holy Spirit and friends who gave him good counsel, and other supportive people, has been an exciting journey from death staring him in the face to his current position, which is as an everlasting saint in God's heavenly Kingdom.

10

WHEN GOD GIVES
A LONG LIFE TO REVIEW

As I sit at my computer musing over my lifetime, there is much to review. What events during all these years are worth relating? There are many decisions to make so that what is written down gives the reader a clear view of how God works His gracious miracles in a very ordinary, poor-to-middle-class woman's life.

To provide an overview of how I feel about my life, I'm including here the first verse of an old hymn, "God Leads us Along."

In shady green pastures so rich and so sweet
God leads His dear children along,
Where the water's cool flow bathes the weary ones feet,
God leads His dear children along,
Some through the waters,
some through the flood,
some through the fire,
but all through the blood.
Some through great sorrow
but God gives a song
in the night seasons
and all the day long.

As with most everyone, each season of life has its happy times and sad times, times of struggle and times of overcoming. Even children experience things like this when their parents teach them day by day, enabling them to learn the basics of living and their place in the world, as well as teaching them about the Lord Jesus who died on the cross to bring salvation to everyone who will ask for it. This chapter tells the moments of my long life that have been most significant to me, many of which have convinced me how gracious and creative God is as He walks with us mortal beings in our brief time on earth. Not everything I'm sharing is a miracle. Some stories are quite mundane, but I think they show how very ordinary I am. And yet God has helped me through everything I have faced. And I'm still growing. Even though I'm 93 this year, I'm still finding new depths of communion with my Savior God, and new adventures in prayer and the transformation of lives around me.

When I was contemplating writing this book, the Holy Spirit gave me the title "Miracles in the Making." What does that mean? In the 1700s, David Hume declared that miracles are impossible because they violate natural laws. At that time, people were feeling the power of knowledge. As European society moved into the 1800s, new philosophies and ideas arose. The Age of Reason, also called The Age of Enlightenment, was full of the new thoughts about the nature of human life, and there was a strong desire to abandon belief in God in favor of the preeminence of human reason and the realities of the natural world. Hume's statement was eagerly embraced and people began to believe in a closed system in which no divine intervention was possible, expected, or required. Many people today believe in this closed system. No external help is forthcoming, so we must do what we can, because this is all there is and all we will ever get.

Is it? My experiences say no. My eyes have seen solutions to huge problems and needs that defy human reason or effort to bring about. But the biggest miracle, by far, is that God Himself, Creator of heaven and earth, became one of us, entering into our sufferings, defeating death, hell, and the grave, and now invites each human being to know Him in a way that is uniquely personal. He cares deeply about our individual lives and wants to communicate with us as friend to Friend. And we can partner with Him in reaching into the sufferings of others, bringing them that same radiant life we have been designed to share with Him.

We do not live in a closed system. Jesus has opened heaven's door so we may talk to God and hear back from Him. We may ask for guidance, help, wisdom, and peace of heart in the midst of the storm. Jesus already intervened in human history, and He will joyfully participate with each of us as we learn to live the abundant life of a human being in divine relationship with the One Who gave us that life.

A lot of living has gone on in these many years, and many of the most significant events to me do not fall within the scope of this book. Regretfully, I have left them out, though an uncut version of my life story has been kept for my family, because my sons, their families, their work, and the times we've had together are precious to me beyond measure. I have also traveled to glorious places on earth, such as New Zealand and Scotland, for God has given me my heart's desires more than once. However this book would be 2000 pages long if I wrote about everything that has been meaningful to me, so I have chosen to let the Holy Spirit be the editor and decide what He would have you know of my faith journey as a member of a family with an extraordinary legacy of faith and faithfulness to the living God, and the evidence of His unrelenting faithfulness to us.

My parents were Percy and Margarette Wills, who lived in Auburn, Washington, with their young son, my brother Frank. Percy pastored a growing church there, but he and Margarette had been praying about a change God seemed to be leading them to make. An answer came in an invitation to join the Shantymen's Christian Association as a missionary to the west coast of Vancouver Island, B.C. They accepted the offer and began preparing to make the move.

Life In Vancouver, B.C.

In June of 1930, just one month after I was born, we moved in with my mother's family who lived in Vancouver, B.C. That was a significant blessing for us because, in this new missionary endeavor, my dad would be away for long periods of time, but Mother, Frank and I would be with family. There would be help for Mother with a new baby, and she would have the support she needed during her recovery after my birth. Mother had a troubling health issue—an overactive thyroid. Doctors had warned her not to have any more children after Frank was born, but she chose to bring me into the world anyway. Maybe that was the first of the miracles in my life. The world said no more children, but God said He had a better idea.

My grandmother, Maggie, lived with her son John and young daughter, Millie, who was Frank's age, as well as a foster girl, Hazel, four years older than me, and a permanent boarder we called Uncle Charlie, who claimed he taught me to walk. We were a close family who loved the Lord and worked together to make it through the Great Depression that had just started in Canada as well as the U.S.

As the economy dropped, there were fewer jobs available, and many families were severely stricken in their pocketbooks. As the months went by, soup lines formed to feed those who had little food and no money to buy any. That went on for several years until the economy began to make a turn and grow instead of decline.

During that time, I don't ever remember not having enough to eat or lacking anything necessary. Uncle John and Uncle Charlie had jobs, so we had money to buy food. Grandma was a very good cook, and even though there were usually nine of us at the table, there seemed always enough food, often including dessert, and no one went hungry. I don't know if the adults were worried because I never heard a word of worry from any of them. Before every meal, one of the adults would always thank the Lord for the food. Perhaps the family prayed to stretch whatever money they had. I don't know. I just know they always gave God credit for the provision and never took it for granted.

My Uncle John had previously had his own business as an electrician, but no one was building, so there wasn't much business in that field. He sometimes got jobs outside Vancouver, and would be gone for several weeks. When that happened, Grandma Maggie would take in another boarder to help with our expenses.

Mother was able to get a job as a secretary in an insurance company. I remember her saying that one man insured by that company paid off a hospital bill at one dollar per month. Since Mother was working, Grandma took over all the household duties, with help from the older children.

Dad spent weeks on the new mission field, then he would come home for a few days. I didn't know what he was doing, only that he was away. The astonishing establishment of Esperanza hospital and caring for the needs of the scattered inhabitants of that perilous coast was full of miracles, but he didn't talk about it when he was home. Looking back, I think he didn't want to take any glory from what he knew God alone could accomplish, but I didn't get to share this part of his life, and if he struggled in his walk of faith, he never told me. He was a kind and thoughtful man, calm, wise, always busy with the Lord's work. I respected and loved him, and I tried my best never to cause any trouble. If I had a need, I didn't tell him. It seemed like he was someone to be good for, instead of a father.

There was one time when my dad was home for quite a while. He was working with boat builders in nearby New Westminster, building the Messenger II, the first boat for the mission. My dad's hands would get bruised from working with the heavy wood as he helped construct the boat. He also helped around the house, cooking and fixing things and spending time with us kids. That Christmas, he and Frank put a jigsaw puzzle together, all but the last piece, which they couldn't find, though they looked all over for it, including the floor. Turns out, I had it and may have been starting to chew on it when my father looked up and saw it in my hand. He wasn't happy about that. It's the only time I recall that he was ever upset with me, but I remember it vividly even today.

While the boat was being built, people came around to see what was going on. Dad told me the kids were very inquisitive, so when the boat was completed, he invited all the kids in the neighborhood to see it. He said they ran all over, looking at the pilot's area where all the controls were, checking out the bunks, the different features of the boat, and the equipment. I didn't know much about what that boat was going to do, but I told my father, "Daddy, I want to pray for blankets for the boat." Dad said that was a good thing to do. I remember not knowing how to pray, so I just said, "Please get blankets" over and over again for a while.

The next night the Shantymen's group held a meeting to tell how God provided the funds for the boat and that it was fully paid for. One woman sat in front and listened raptly to the story. At the end of the meeting, she stood and said to the crowd, "I came to Victoria to play winter golf, but this has made such an impact on me that I would like to have a part in this boat." She said she would give the treasurer a check for $25.00, a significant amount then, and added that she would like the money to go for the bedding for the boat. Dad was struck by this quick answer to his daughter's prayer and the whole group praised God for this gift.

The Messenger II was dedicated to mission service in 1934. I sat on the grassy field with family members watching the service when the boat was commissioned. I was only four at the time, so the significance was lost on me, but I remember the event and how happy my parents were.

I was still pretty young when Mom, Dad, Uncle John, and Grandma pooled their resources and bought a larger house not far from where we had been living. I heard that it cost them eight hundred dollars. It was on a big lot, had a full basement, two floors, plus an attic with a lot of space. A streetcar a couple of blocks away provided transportation for those working.

There were kids in the neighborhood and we played games such as Hide and Seek and Hopscotch with the squares drawn in chalk on the sidewalk. We had a pair of roller skates that were a Christmas present. We shared them, with each person having one skate. For Frank and Millie, Dad took a short board and attached hockey pucks for wheels. The pucks were round and made of very hard rubber. His invention worked really well—an early version of a skate board. He tried to patent it, but it was too futuristic for that time.

On Sundays our family attended the local Foursquare Church. We children walked there for Sunday School and the adults joined us later for the services. The pastor was a woman, Anna D. Britton, who was noted for her prayer life. Someone told her I could sing and she invited me to sing one Sunday morning. They had to put a box behind the pulpit for me to stand on so I could be seen. I guess it went well for I was invited a few times more.

Our spiritual life was also developed at home. We heard Bible stories and were guided by our elders in the ways of God. Mother, or Dad when he was home, would read the Bible to me at bedtime. When I could read, I was encouraged to read it for myself. It was not a children's Bible; it was standard King James. I didn't understand everything, but I didn't know the nutritional value of the food I ate every day either. Still, I was taught early to respect and read the

Bible as a vital part of my life, and I grew up nourished with the Word of God, which my parents obviously considered to be such an essential part of our lives.

From my earliest days, prayer has been a big factor in my life. I had some awareness of God and said my prayers at night. I'm sure that living in a family that honored God every day was a founding part of that, as well as praying for my father when he was away from home for several weeks at a time, even though I had no knowledge of the dangers he experienced while he was ministering on the treacherous west coast of Vancouver Island.

I don't know if my early case of pneumonia affected my immune system, or if the other children were bringing home germs from school. I was very thin and caught whatever diseases were going around. One time I had the measles. In those days when that happened, a family doctor would put a Quarantine notice on the front door as a warning.

I was put to bed with the blinds drawn to darken the room as a shield for my eyes. At that time the medical profession thought the eyes could be affected by the bright light of day. But the day was long lying in bed, except for the time Grandma came to check on me. What could I do? This was before I went to school, but I had learned to read and do simple arithmetic from watching the other kids do their homework. I got a book and started reading, even in the dark room. I hid the book under the covers whenever Mother or Grandma brought me something. I recovered without any problems with my eyes.

When I was six, I started walking to school with Millie, Frank, and Hazel. I went into first grade, the starting point of education then. Soon after I began, the teacher saw that I could read well and do some arithmetic, so I was advanced to grade two. School was pretty easy for me with the start I had at home.

In the evenings, Mother and Grandma would sit and listen to the radio while they relaxed, doing embroidery work on pillow cases, or crocheting other items. There were times when I couldn't go to sleep for a while, and hearing the radio on, I would get up and sit on the steps of the landing where I could see into the living room. I kept very quiet because I wanted to hear the funny things they were laughing at. I don't remember ever getting caught.

Mother became concerned about my low weight and thin frame, and she started praying for me about it. A few months later a visiting minister came to our church who was considered to have a gift of healing. Mother asked him if he would come to our home and pray for me. I remember him asking the Lord to "Put meat on my bones" and other things meaningful to all of us in the family. From that day on, I began to gain weight and grow at a normal rate.

LIFE IN VICTORIA, B.C.

The next year, in September 1939, Germany declared war on Britain. Britain was a Commonwealth which meant that every one of its countries was also at war, including Canada. Dad left his mission field and went to join the army but he was told he was too old. Later, he heard about a group called Soldier's and Airmen's Christian Association (SACA) that was starting up to provide places where military people could gather in a Christian atmosphere. Otherwise they would have no other opportunities for recreation beside spending time in the local bars.

Dad joined the SACA and established his ministry in Victoria, the Provincial capital and a military city with bases for the Army, Navy, and Air Force. He found just the right place for the ministry to the service people—a big home on a double lot, with ample rooms for family and entertaining copious numbers of people for a few hours, or even a few days. He rented it for 50 dollars a month.

Dad, Mother, and I moved to Victoria right after school was out in June. My brother Frank enlisted in the Air Force and was sent to a base in one of the prairie provinces. Victoria was Dad's home town, so we traded one family for another. His father and mother, Frank and Annie, with their daughter Amy, lived together and other family members lived in the area.

This move began the next phase of my life—mainly my formative teen years. It was the first time that my dad was home all the time, every day. In the mornings, Dad would come into my room, shut the window, and tell me it was time to get up. While I was getting ready, he would be preparing breakfast for me. He was pretty careful with Mom to make sure she got enough rest. I have a picture of him with an apron on and kitchen towel slung over his shoulder. He was involved in everything and he kept an eye on everything.

For me, this was a time of learning to know Jesus, growing up in faith, getting involved in church, and beginning my musical education.

It didn't take long for news to get around the military bases that there was a really nice home where they could go when they had some free time from base. Almost immediately after we were settled in the house, we were plunged into this new work for the Lord. Dad named the house Emmaeus, which means, "God with us." He surely was, because He provided so well that there was always enough provisions for food, bedding, and strength to handle all the chores, some of which we had to learn. One of them was how to make a dinner for, say, six, and stretch it to feed 9. It always worked, though.

One of the features of the house that I really liked was the arrangement of the two bedrooms occupied by me and my parents. They were at the front of the house and were connected by an enclosed sun porch. In the summer time Dad put a cot in there for me to sleep on. I loved it because I would open the big windows and look out on the sky and stars until I went to sleep.

In the winters with the rain and heavy winds blowing, I would snuggle in my blankets and listen to the rain on the roof. If it was foggy weather, I would hear the mournful sounds of the fog horns. The combination would lull me to sleep.

This was also a dream place for a young, teenage girl. Every day there were "cute" guys in the home who were in their late teens and early 20s. There were a few I thought would be fun to be with. One actually invited me to go roller skating. Dad said I could go with him and told me he would go and watch me until I fell. I made sure I didn't fall. I had no idea my dad was chaperoning me.

As you can imagine, there was a lot of cooking, cleaning, laundry, and all things necessary to have a place ready for people to come. One of my duties was to peel the vegetables for supper when I got home from school. Both Mother and Dad were excellent cooks, and our meals were so appreciated by the guys as a treat from the military mess on base.

On Saturdays, I had some cleaning duties plus making the cots ready for the men who could stay overnight. Mother spent the morning baking several batches of cookies, which would be quickly devoured.

The door of Emmaeus was always open to anyone who wanted to come, and no charges were ever made for food or an overnight stay. Dad had monthly support from the SACA for this place, but I never knew how much it was. We didn't know what the expenses would be for each month. It truly was a faith-based work for the Lord, to show His love to the men and women who would soon be on the battlefield.

Dad made sure that Jesus was made known to all who came. The men found that my dad was loving and caring for their souls. They could ask him questions they didn't have answers for, and he would respect whatever they asked and give them an answer that made sense to them. Many a young man came to trust Jesus as Savior because my dad knew when to speak to their souls, and when just to pray for them. Dad seemed to know when someone was troubled, and would engage him in conversation designed to ease his fears. The guy's face would brighten and he would walk away with a smile on his face.

Dad had house rules, too, concerning certain words about women (such as "tomato"), or arguing about whatever was in the news. He did allow some pranks, as long as they were just simple ones. He did not allow arguments on religious issues, such as eternal security of believers. He said the Bible said that "Whoever believes in the Son of God has life" (1 John 5:12) and pointed out that it was in the present tense.

Living in this atmosphere of faith in a God Who supplied liberally, and seeing the results of that faith, was a great lesson to me that was more "caught than taught." I think I absorbed it, and it was a sense of trust in God that became a bedrock of my own growing faith.

Not only was I in a new city, I was going to a new school, into Grade 6. The first day I sat in class, the teacher asked each of us our names. When he got to me I said that my name was Darda. I had to repeat it two or three times and I began to wonder about this man who could not say such a simple name. What kind of teacher could he be? So I decided since he couldn't handle Darda, I would give him my middle name. Slowly and clearly, I said, "My name is Jean," which I pronounced distinctly to make sure he understood what I was saying, "Jean." I figured he couldn't mess that one up.

I had started taking music lessons when we lived in Vancouver, and after we moved to Victoria, I continued with a new teacher, a wonderful Christian woman. She taught piano and voice, and I was her student all the time I lived there. She put me in a program from the Royal Conservatory of Toronto, a correspondence course that one could follow and gain a degree in teaching piano. There were lessons throughout the year and every year they would send their music teachers out to check on the students. You could make an appointment and be tested on what you'd been learning that year. You would get the report to show you where your weaknesses were and whether you had passed the exam.

When I was twelve, a Chinese evangelist named Mun Hope visited our home. That evening, he asked me if I had ever asked Jesus to be my Savior. I seemed to have a sense of God, but I had never specifically asked Him to save me. Mr. Hope led me to do just that.

Right after that I went to Dad and told him what I had just done. He sat me on his lap put his arm around me and talked to me about the meaning of what I had done. After that I told Mother that I had accepted Jesus. To me, it seemed to complete something that had already been started a long time before.

We found a new church in downtown Victoria and spent our Sundays at their services. I joined their choir. Because we had so many servicemen coming who may or may not know about Jesus, Dad thought that having an after-meeting gathering on Sunday nights and inviting the young people of the various churches to come for an hour or so, would help the men interact with other young people who were Christians. He announced to those churches that after their evening service we would have a Sing Song time from about 8 p.m. to 10 p.m. For the first few weeks the people from each church would sit together, but soon, as they got acquainted with those from other churches, you couldn't tell which church they represented.

It didn't take long for the living room and adjoining areas to be filled with young people who enjoyed singing choruses, or hymns. There was always somebody who could play the piano. Whenever we got a letter from someone who had been sent to another military base, Dad would read the letter so we all could know how that person was faring. Others who had found the Lord would tell their testimony of salvation, or how God met a need they had requested prayer for.

Then there was coffee that Dad boiled in a huge vat-type pan. He would add an egg shell to settle the grounds, and serve it up. There were cookies that Mother had made the day before, along with slices of a loaf cake that Dad's sister, Bessie, sent. Some of the guys would help in the serving.

I tried to hide among the people in the crowd so Dad couldn't see me and send me to bed. I loved being where things were going on, but he usually spotted me. When he caught my eye, he would put his two hands together at the side of his tilted head. That was my signal to get upstairs and go to bed. School was the next day.

Being in such an enjoyable time with people of different denominations, from different parts of the country, and different military forces was another foundational lesson to me. I saw that people of many denominations could be friends with other denominations, as long as both loved and worshiped Jesus. I also learned to get along with, and appreciate, people who had a wide range of temperaments, of various habits and world views. That lesson has helped me to this day, to treat others with respect and kindness, even if I don't agree with them.

Another thing that Dad started was a monthly Fun Night. The war was so much on people's minds, some with loved ones on the battlefield, or who had just received notice that their son or father was killed, or Missing in Action. He wanted to bring some light humor into the house. Once a month the people could come for games, fun, and, of course, coffee and cookies.

One of these nights just before Christmas the house was crowded with people. As they were getting ready to leave, someone hung a sprig of mistletoe above the front door. Several of the guys lined up on the porch so that every girl leaving could get a kiss. Everyone was laughing and cheering, including me. In fact, I was hollering so much that I made myself hoarse for the next several days.

Christmas was always a special time for us all. We put up and decorated a good-sized tree. At Emmaeus, socks were attached to the mantle over the fire place, one for every person who would be there Christmas morning. Gift packages were stacked under the tree ready to be opened after breakfast.

This one Christmas morning as we sat in the living room opening our presents, there were lots of "oohs" and "ahs", "thank you's" and words of appreciation. Except for Dad. Every gift he opened was a box of handkerchiefs. After opening several such boxes, he exclaimed for the next one, "More snot rags." I think there was one gift that was different, but I don't remember what it was.

Another very special time was the wedding for Mother's sister, my aunt Millie, and her fiance, an airforce man named Milton Bryans. The wedding day was set for November 4, 1943. He was stationed in the Aleutian Islands and arranged to get leave for his wedding, which would take place at our house with Dad officiating.

Because of rationing, Mother worked hard to gather enough ingredients to make a proper meal for the reception. I think the wedding cake was ordered from a bakery. Milton asked some of his friends to take part in the wedding, and Millie asked me to be her bridesmaid. One of her friends was her Maid of Honor.

Two days before the wedding, a telegram came from Milton that there was stormy weather at his base and he couldn't fly out. That caused quite a stir at home as to what to do about the food that was being prepared. What do we do? Do we eat it or can it be preserved? We did not know how long the interval would be. Mother decided to keep it as fresh as possible for the present time.

A couple of days later, Milton wired that he could fly out and be in Victoria on the 6th of November. Everyone let out the breath they had been holding, and preparations for the wedding went back on. The servicemen who were a part of the wedding party were able to get their leaves adjusted so they could still stand up with Milton.

On the evening of the 6th, Milton and his best man stood at the fireplace waiting for Millie to appear. She wore a long white wedding dress, and her Maid of Honor and I were in long dresses of pale blue with embroidered flowers on the skirt. I felt grown up in mine.

Dad read the wedding vows and then he blessed them with a short talk encouraging Milton to be the head of the house and for Millie to take her place by his side as his partner. As I stood there in my beautiful long dress listening to what Dad was saying, and hearing the vows that were spoken to each other, it was sobering to me to realize the solemnity of the wedding vows in a marriage.

The reception was in our dining room, the table laden with the meal that Mother and Dad had prepared. In spite of the delay in the wedding, all of that carefully collected and prepared food was fresh and delicious.

The next fall I started high school. You could choose courses leading to college, or courses preparing boys and girls for jobs once they graduated. I chose the one for college preparation.

About three years after we were involved in this ministry, Mother was getting quite weary with the constant work and people coming and going in such numbers. She needed a vacation, but Dad had no idea where she could go, nor how to pay for it.

Once more, God stepped in and supplied the provision. Michael Billester was holding meetings in Victoria. He was a Russian missionary and the founder of the Refugee Evangelistic Mission, and my dad knew him well. Dad talked his dilemma over with him. Michael said that as soon as these meetings were over he was driving home to California. He could take Mother and me for a week's stay with his family, and we would return by bus. With a grateful heart, Dad accepted his offer.

Mother and I fully enjoyed the road trip and the different scenery along the way. We were on Highway 99, seeing the lumber mills of Southern Oregon, lakes and rivers, a big lake, and magnificent Mount Shasta and the mountains of Northern California—roads twisting and turning, which was new for me. I hadn't seen anything like that.

Michael and his family lived in El Monte in California's San Gabriel Valley, but they went to a church in Hollywood because they knew the pastor. We arrived in Los Angeles on Good Friday. Michael had arranged for us all to meet at their church in Hollywood for the evening service. When we arrived, he introduced us to his wife Amanda, and their son, Robert. We all enjoyed the service, then got ready to drive back to their home for the week.

Michael was driving a coupe that held only three people so he drove Amanda and Mother. Their son Robert had driven his mother to the church, but she was riding with Mother and Michael, so there was room in his car for a passenger—me. I rode to their home in his car.

Robert was four years older than me, and I was used to being around teenaged guys that age, so I wasn't particularly impressed that I was alone with him. I was more taken with the car than with Robert. We called it the Tomato Can because it was the color of cream of tomato soup and it had one of those horns that went "Awooga."

The family lived in a very nice ranch-style home with big rooms and a treated cement floor. It had actually been featured in one of the home magazines. It had a nice front yard with a lot of trees and a climbing rose bush. There was a walnut tree, a persimmon tree, and, on either side of the gate to their property, a grapefruit tree.

Mother and I spent a lovely week with them, and got acquainted with Amanda's mother we called Grandma Barr. We were so happy to have beautiful sunny, warm days instead of the cool, cloudy gray April days up north. We were treated with such kindness for that week. They put themselves out to show us the good tourist places there. Then Michael put Mother and me on a bus and sent us on our way. We were glad to be home after that refreshing time away from the hurry and scurry of daily life in Victoria. Then both Mother and I resumed our daily routine once more.

Maybe a year or so later, I was awakened during the night by some activity in my parent's bedroom that adjoined mine. I got up to see what was happening. My mother was having trouble breathing, and Dad was up caring for her. Dad was very collected just like he would be during the day. When Mom was gasping and saying, "I can't breathe," he didn't seem upset or nervous. One moment she was too warm and Dad opened the window. Then she got cold, so he closed it. Dad saw me there and told me quietly just to go back to bed. He didn't seem flustered at all. He was very composed as he always was, so I was not alarmed and went back to my room.

Mother was having a heart attack, as a result of her overactive thyroid. The doctor sent her to a hospital in Vancouver for surgery. I traveled with her and stayed with my grandmother while she was hospitalized.

Mother's condition was so serious that she was kept in bed for ten days before surgery was attempted. She could not read a newspaper, listen to a radio, or do anything else that could alarm her emotional state. When she was finally taken to the operating room, they cooled her temperature down so she would not need as much anaesthetic. Her thyroid gland was removed. When she was discharged from the hospital she recovered at Grandmother's home.

I remember vividly one warm summer day when I came into the house to cool off, there was Mother lying on the couch in her flannel pajamas, covered in a down quilt, a hot water bottle at her feet. It made me feel hot just looking at her encased in blankets. I was too young to realize the severity of her condition.

While Mother and I were in Vancouver, my aunt Millie went to Victoria to help Dad out with the daily chores. Other friends also volunteered so that the work could continue to keep Emmaeus open for the servicemen. God made sure that things went as smoothly as possible during our time away.

When Mother and I returned home, there was a great welcome for us and much love shown as we resumed our places in the daily activities. Dad was very careful of Mother and made sure she got enough rest while she took up the things she did in her usual routine.

A few months later, the Allied forces in Europe were winning against Germany and Italy. In the final days France, Belgium, and the Netherlands were freed from their bondage under the heavy foot of the German forces.

In one of my science classes the teacher told us that the atom was the smallest thing that could not be split. Little did we know that it had not only been split, it had been made into a very lethal bomb that was instrumental in ending the war against Japan in the Pacific.

Once the war ended, there were far fewer military men coming to the house. We had one final, very special dinner at the end of the year right after Christmas. God brought to our home a group of missionaries who had been freed from a Japanese prison camp where they had been confined for four years. We were honored to have them join our other guests for a truly memorable meal. It was a tremendous closure to six years of ministry to the servicemen and women who passed through our doors and our hearts.

Even before we left the big house on Belmont Avenue, my parents were praying and considering what they should do about their housing—rent, or buy? The Lord gave them an answer through friends, who suggested they build a home. Their friends told them there was a nice lot for sale only a few houses away from them, and they offered the use of the blueprints for their home, which was a nice floor plan for a two-story, two-bedroom home. Not only that, but a building contractor lived just around the corner from this lot. When Dad contacted him, he agreed to build the house for them. He even finished the attic so we could put extra beds up there for family use. The neighborhood was a quiet one with nicely kept homes and gardens to look at. The house was right next door to a grocery store, a little fish and chip shop, and a drugstore. There was a bus stop on the corner for our transportation into town when Dad was away. I could ride my bike to the high school to finish out my senior year. My brother Frank was discharged from the Air Force and moved in with us. Once again, our family was together, and a new stage of life began for the four of us.

It was quite an adjustment after six years of daily work preparing for the constant coming and going of military service personnel who ate and slept in our home 24/7. Back then, it was a rare day when my parents and I were alone.

I enjoyed our new home and really liked my bedroom where I could sit at a desk and do homework. The view out of the window was pleasant with a big green yard and a large willow tree that spread its branches so that one could sit under it in the summer and have shade.

My parents were very hospitable and their home became the hub of many activities related to the mission and their church.

They were still in frequent contact with many of the military men and women who had been such a large part of their lives during the war.

My father was glad to resume his boat ministry to the Shantymen, and he and Harold Peters, who had become a missionary towards the end of the war, went out to minister on a boat, and Doc McLean went in Messenger II to bring medical help and encouragement from God.

Weather on the coast is violent and unpredictable, and these men were literally taking their lives in their hands every time they went out on their boats to minister to the people there. One time my dad and Harold were on one boat while Doc and his son Bruce were returning in Messenger II from where it had been harbored during storms that made it unsafe to be on the water. We always had a background awareness of the risks they were taking, and on that one trip, fifteen-year-old Bruce was washed overboard and drowned. Belonging to God doesn't mean He will always keep you from drowning when you are a young person not yet far on life's journey, but one of the most important aspects of the Christian life is the knowledge that this brief time on earth is not all there is. There is a reunion ahead of us where we will never again be parted from those who have gone ahead. When Bruce was lost, our grief was sharp and deep, but we knew he was safely with Jesus. It makes me wonder how people who do not have that assurance can survive the loss of anyone, much less the death of a child. The missionaries made sure the people they served knew Jesus loved them, heaven is real, and they could be certain they would go there and be with Him forever.

Because of my dad's work with the Shantymen, I heard so many stories of God's presence in dangers or dire need, that I came to expect that personal involvement as a normal part of the Christian life. I have found it truly is the norm, but many of God's children don't know that. My dad's stories helped them see the reality from an eyewitness, and the people loved it. They were eager to hear him tell about the mission work, and I loved how they responded when he told those stories. Hearing about real dangers and real provision, help, and deliverance opened the eyes of those living lives where the miraculous was not expected because they didn't know God was still doing such things in this modern day and age. In this way, my dad and the other missionaries opened new vistas to listeners of what the Christian life is meant to be, with the assurance that God wanted to intervene in their own storms and dangers with the same grace and love as He provided for the missionaries.

On one of the times when Dad was invited to tell about the mission work, Mother and I went with him to a church located up-island. We always enjoyed his talks of how God provided for whatever need there was, and when people were born again. Dad always made sure that God was given full credit for the results of the work done.

I don't remember the town, or what Dad talked about. All I remember is the response I came away with. On the drive home I sat in a deep sense of quietness. I knew it was of God. I didn't want to talk nor listen to what was being said by Mother and Dad. I wasn't looking at the scenery. I didn't want to lose the great sense of peace I had that lasted for the rest of the drive home.

Dad was on the boats till he was told by the doctor that he couldn't be on the boat anymore. He continued to serve the mission with administrative work and in an advisory capacity and was available for talks to churches and other groups, telling about the work that was currently being done at Esperanza and the expansion of the ministry that was to include summer camps for the children. As time went by, he also help establish a couple of other ministries on the island. That was after I married and moved to Southern California. After that I lost track of what the mission was doing.

Without the endless cooking and cleaning and ministry that she did in Emmaeus, Mother actually had free time. But rather than rest and relax or take up an enjoyable hobby, she got a part time job as a secretary to the manager of the Provincial Government Employee's Association. She was an excellent typist and the only one I knew who could type a document while carrying on a conversation at the same time. That was on the older typewriters where you typed a line, then hit a bar that would move the carriage to the left to type the next line, and so on, line by line until you finished the whole document.

I graduated from high school that June, but continued with my music lessons. I was learning about music history, composition, and a thing called counterpoint that may have been a part of learning to compose music. Each one of those required passing a 3 hour exam. I did pass those. That meant I was now fully qualified to teach piano. Otherwise, I had no clue about what line of work I would begin to learn. I prayed about it, but nothing came to mind. I heard about being a Lab Technician, and that sounded interesting, but when I looked into it, all doors closed, so I dropped that possibility.

It was about this time that Robert Billester came back into my life. He had visited a couple of times before when Michael was holding meetings, but this time he was in Victoria for a longer period. He stayed at the YMCA in town and he and I had time to get to know each other better. Mother and Dad also got to know him, and allowed me to go with him to various places during the day.

One time we went on a walk and were sitting on a park bench. There were some children playing nearby and Bob got up and talked to them. I thought, "Oh, that's a nice thing that he paid attention to them."

As well as being a serious Bible student, Bob was fun to be with. He had a great sense of humor. We would both laugh at the same things. And he could do imitations of people. His family had a dog that was a mixture of bulldog and Scotty. Bob would put Woggie on his lap and talk like they were having a conversation. He was also a musician. He played the piano and the trumpet.

Bob was tall—almost six feet—and stocky like his father (who was Russian), but surprisingly agile at the same time. He had brown hair and a gentle demeanor. He was very close to his mother, of course, because his dad was gone for long periods of time and so was mine. He was kind and caring with his mother and grandmother, a thoughtful person who watched out for the well-being of others. But most importantly, he loved Jesus, knew his Bible, and he acted like it.

Bob told us that God called him to the ministry. I'm sure his father hoped that he would join their mission, but Bob needed training before making any such decision. He returned to his home in El Monte before moving to Bob Jones University for his freshman year. Back then, the campus was in Tennessee. He signed up for courses in their "Preacher Boy's" discipline to begin his training for ministry. We wrote to each other to keep in contact while we were apart.

There must have been something brewing in me because I felt a loyalty to him. I was told later on he had spoken to one of his friends and said he was going to marry me. That was after we came back from visiting his family when I was 14.

As I got to know what Bob was like as a person, I started to love him. The love just sort of built up. I believe that God had put him in my life. God had chosen Bob to be my husband but we lived 1200 miles apart, and that extended time when Bob was in Victoria was the way God gave us a chance to develop the relationship that would need to be strong for all the changes and storms ahead.

In Victoria, I entered Victoria College, taking the usual basic freshman courses and keeping up with my music lessons and practice times. In the evenings I was active with the young people at church, and began leading the choir.

When my freshman year was over, I dropped out because I didn't know what type of career I wanted to train for. At the same time, Bob found that he was not satisfied with the classes he had at Bob Jones University, so he dropped out there and returned home. We continued our correspondence.

I decided to get a job and Mother told me the Motor Vehicle Department in the Provincial government had an opening for a clerk. So I applied, and was hired. My salary was $98.00 a month. After six months, since it was a government office, I would have to declare my allegiance to the King. I did not want to do that and possibly lose my American citizenship. I resigned and spent the time preparing for my music exams.

When Bob proposed marriage to me I said "Yes." One thing Bob forgot was to ask Mother and Dad. The error caused a bit of a stir. Mother's concern, and it was a valid one, was that I had not dated anyone, and did not have enough life-time experience, or even a job, in case I needed to work. She wanted me to spend more time enjoying life as a single person. Dad did not give his opinion to me at all. I guess he left that to Mother.

Of course, I had answers to Mother's concerns. I was in love with Bob, and I had my music in case I needed to work. If I was to move away from home, why not have my own house instead of renting from somebody else in a strange town? I felt it was God's timing for me.

I was only 19, but it was not considered young in those days. A lot of girls would graduate from high school, get engaged, and get married. My mother's mother had married at 15, so she thought it was perfectly fine for me to marry Bob. Mom eventually agreed, things got worked out, and our engagement was announced.

Since we had not spent a lot of time together, I decided to take a trip to visit Bob at his home in El Monte, and get to know him and his parents. It was a good decision, and when I returned home I felt more secure in looking forward to being a part of them as a daughter-in-law.

From the time I was a young girl, I wanted to get married and have a family. It was so important to me that I prayed that Jesus would not come back to earth until after I had achieved that goal. Now here I was, engaged to a godly young man and plans were being made to fulfill that dream.

I have heard that sometimes when God is going to do something special in the future, He will give an early "sign,"(as in signs and wonders) as a portent of what He will do later on. I have come to think that my unusual meeting with Bob while Mother and I were on a simple vacation, was a sort of sign that he would be my husband when we were old enough to marry.

Even though I had not dated at all, and there were some nice young men at church, the Lord brought to me the man of His choice. Apparently, none of the local men met His requirements. Yet, in His wisdom, He brought this young man into my life when I was fourteen years old. During the whole time I lived in Victoria, Bob moved around a few times until I was ready for this very serious step.

Mother's talents included her abilities as a seamstress. She made a nightgown and robe set for me, several dresses, and a beautiful ivory satin wedding gown, At the neckline, she added a lovely lace collar.

There's a story about that collar that I want to include here. When Dad was in the military in France with his brother Archie, his brother was collecting this Valenciennes lace and he left some of it with Dad and asked him to bring it with him when he went home. One piece was a collar that was shoulder width and went from neckline to shoulder all around. Someone stole all of it but that collar, and somehow my dad brought that collar back and gave it to me. That's what I heard. My mother attached the Valenciennes lace to my wedding dress. And I still have it.

The wedding date was set for July 11, 1949. Because Dad and Mother were so well known, it was a large wedding. I asked Dad to be a part of the ceremony, so my Uncle John was the one who walked me down the aisle. I guess he thought I was in a hurry, because he told me to slow down. Bob, with my brother Frank as his Best Man, and my Matron of Honor, my dear friend Julia, with other attendants, were waiting at the front with Dad and my pastor. It was a solemn time for Bob and me as we repeated our vows in the middle of the happiest day of our lives.

It was very hard to say good-bye to Mother and Dad and see their eyes full of tears. We knew we would not see each other again for many months. There were long, strong hugs and many kisses before we all wiped our eyes, and Bob and I started the long drive to Southern California.

A couple of days later, we arrived at Bob's home, and moved into a studio apartment in a separate building on the property where his parents lived. It was our home for the next few years until we built our own home next door.

LIVING IN SOUTHERN CALIFORNIA

Now that I was no longer in the Godly influence of my parents, I had to develop my own faith in the Lord according to what I read in the Bible. I was married and living far from my parents in a totally different world. It was a huge adjustment for me and I'm not talking only about being married. First was the climate. I was not used to daytime temperatures of 100+ degrees. One day in November it was 103. Then there was the traffic. El Monte was a suburb in the L.A. basin. Even at that time you could drive almost a hundred miles and still be in suburban traffic. Back in the 1950s, the freeways were just starting to be built.

Then there was getting used to the ways of a new family. Even though our apartment was separate, we ate our meals in their home. Bob's grandmother, Grandma Barr, helped take care of the house and meals while his mother attended to the business side of their work, Refugee Evangelistic Mission. Bob's father could be away for a few months, driving across Canada and the U.S. speaking at various churches telling about their work among the Slavic people in Europe and South America. Occasionally Michael visited their missionaries in those countries.

I wrote letters to Mother and Dad to let them know how I was and what we were doing. Occasionally, they would phone us and tell us what was going on with my family and assure us that they were praying for us. It was so good to hear their voices and I could tell they missed me as much as I missed them. I was only 19 and I'm sure they worried about how I would do missing them and home and trying to make a new life in totally different circumstances.

The previous year, Bob had enrolled in BIOLA, the Bible Institute of Los Angeles, and I started that September 1949, in the Music Department. I was so happy to be attending BIOLA because in Victoria I had often listened to their radio broadcasts, and thought how nice it would be to go there. Now here I was, actually walking in the door, finding my classroom, and waiting for the professor to start the lecture. I was so thankful that God had worked that desire out.

Our daily ritual began with driving the several miles to downtown L.A., finding a parking place, and getting to class on time. Each student had to be involved in a Christian work of some kind and give a report on what they did each week. Bob and I began to work with the young people of the Russian Church in L.A.

Another stipulation was that every freshman had to join the choir and attend a practice after school once or twice a week. That really upset our schedule, for Bob had to wait for me before we could go home. That problem was solved when we learned there was streetcar service from L.A. to El Monte. I could walk to the streetcar station, and walk a few blocks home when I arrived at my stop.

Not long after I began traveling on the streetcar, I started talking to another passenger. She, too, was a student at BIOLA and she lived only a couple of blocks from me. Bob and I became very good friends with her and her brother, who had been a student at BIOLA. That friendship lasted until a few months ago, when I learned that she had died.

The professors were highly recognized men of God. I felt so privileged to have two years of Bible classes taught by Dr. J. Vernon McGee, the pastor of Church of the Open Door, where BIOLA was based. He can still be heard on the radio program "Thru the Bible." In that period of time he covered the entire Bible.

Once a week there was a chapel time in the morning when the whole student body worshiped together. One morning during the chapel service, the speaker gave an invitation for anyone who wanted to dedicate their life to God. I felt led to respond as I didn't know if I had ever done that. I walked to the front where the speaker prayed for all of us standing there. Later that day I took as my life verse Colossians 1:18b, "…That in everything He might be preeminent." At that time I didn't realize the scope of that verse, but I have tried to live up to it.

In June of 1951, I graduated from BIOLA with a degree in Sacred Music. BIOLA was Bible-based. By the time we graduated, Bob and I had received a good solid training in our walk of faith.

The big news before my graduation was learning that I was pregnant. We were so happy we couldn't keep the smiles off our faces. Our parents were now looking forward to their first grandchild. Our baby boy, whom we named Stephen Edmund Michael Billester, was born healthy and miraculous. We were so proud and grateful for this beautiful child. Later, we had him dedicated to the Lord at the church in Hollywood where Bob and I first met.

That fall, BIOLA announced that it had met the requirements to be a university, and would now offer four-year courses. Bob decided he would transfer to this opportunity, and enrolled for those classes.

Some time later in the fall semester when Bob and I arrived at school one morning, we noticed that the Placement Office door was open and when the manager saw us he motioned for us to join him. We were very curious about what he wanted from us. He got right to the point, telling us that a small group of people in Loma Linda, CA, wanted a student pastor for a new church they started. Were we interested? We were speechless. Didn't know what to say. He said to think and pray about it and let him know what we decided. We left the office in a daze.

Before we were married, Bob had received a call to the ministry, and was ordained by the pastor of the church we were attending. Bob had not been thinking of pastoral work, but more of evangelism. He had actually spent two summers with two other budding ministers touring churches in Canada under the auspices of the great People's Church in Toronto, whose pastor was Oswald J. Smith, a widely known and respected man of God. He and his church heavily focused and supported a whole range of different Christian missions.

Bob and I prayed seriously about this offer. We discussed it with both sets of parents. We remembered those months of Bob's training in ministry, and the new classes available in such a timely manner, and decided the Lord was leading us in this new direction. We drove out to Loma Linda to meet the people who made the request. It was a small group, but they were serious about starting a church, and we told them that we would begin services starting the next month. Bob did the preaching and I provided the music for the meetings.

We got to practice our foundation in faith when we accepted that pastorate for that new church in Loma Linda, a town an hour's drive from home. At that time Bob was still taking classes at BIOLA. We had to lean heavily on the Lord for His help in Bob's preparing his sermons and the work load to maintain his studies at a high level and my taking care of the music on top of the needs of a new baby. At times, the load was almost too much to handle, and our faith was stretched to trust that God would carry us through that period of struggle.

Michael and Amanda were a big help in getting the church organized. Amanda helped us write out the doctrinal statement for the church, and got the church registered with the State of

California. Michael would preach occasionally, and the people truly enjoyed his messages.

The church was growing, but the responsibility of ministering to them began to weigh heavily on us. We felt inadequate to minister spiritually to the people we did not know yet, even though they were kind and receptive to Bob's preaching.

One night we started talking about our doubts, and wondered if there was more to our faith than what we had. We questioned if what we had was all there was? We decided to pray to God for His help and understanding, and were determined to pray until something happened. Our prayers went on for some time when suddenly we were so filled with praise and joy that we couldn't stop worshiping Him. It was a wonderful experience. Unfortunately, it lasted for only a few days because we didn't know what God had done. Eighteen years later, when the Holy Spirit came upon the young people in a new awakening, we learned that, in answer to our prayers in the early days of our ministry, God had given us His Holy Spirit.

Things were going well. We had served in Loma Linda a year and a half, and the Lord had helped us nurture the fledgling flock, even throughout the time of Bob's heavy load of classes and pastoral duties. But it became evident that we could not continue at the church without moving there for full-time ministry. At the same time, we knew we couldn't leave Amanda and Grandma Barr alone since Michael could be gone for long periods of time. Because of that, we decided to resign from the church and stay in El Monte.

Michael and Amanda hoped that Bob would join their mission and eventually take it over when they retired. Michael planned to visit his missionaries in Europe during the summer and invited Bob to go with him. I thought that was a great opportunity for me to have a nice long visit with Mother and Dad so they could meet their new grandson. Our trips were well timed. Within a few days of each other, Michael and Bob were driving off heading for Europe, and I was on the train heading for Victoria.

It was so good to be with Mother and Dad again, to see my brother and meet his new wife Eileen, and visit with my friends. Steve was about 7 months old and a really good baby, especially in a new unknown situation. My parents were happy to babysit for me so I could spend time with my friends during the day.

Almost immediately I settled back into my former routine at home. I became a daughter of the house again, while my folks made the major decisions of the day. They were so proud to show Steve off when people came to visit, or when we visited other relatives in town. Mother and I got to do shopping trips together, which was fun, and I got a few new items to expand my wardrobe.

Meanwhile, over on the other side of the world, Michael and Bob were having a blessed time wherever they held services. The meetings were crowded, and Bob had a real look at how important the impact was that his father had on the people. He learned that if you couldn't preach for at least and hour or more, you were not much of a preacher. He was also introduced to believers who loved the Lord as much as he did but in other cultures, and they welcomed him and showed respect for who he was.

After Michael returned home we talked with them about our housing—we were outgrowing it, for we were expecting another child. I had looked around to see what was available for our needs, but it didn't take long to see most ads for homes were above our ability to buy one.

The home Michael and Amanda owned was on a one acre corner lot. They were able to deed the back one-third of it to us. It was a very loving and generous gesture. We saw a model home of a small 3-bedroom floor plan that was in our price range, and so we had one built on the new lot. The best part of this plan was that we would still be very close and available to Amanda and Grandma Barr when Michael was away on one of his missions or fund-raising trips.

Sandwiched in between the house being built and the coming offer from a new church, our second son, Dale Cameron Billester, was born. He was in a hurry—we just made it to the hospital in time. Now we had another beautiful baby boy, a brand-new life, another of God's miracles.

Although Bob was officially on Michael's mission staff, there were not a lot of things he would be involved in or be paid to do. We had also taken on a financial debt with the house. As we prayed about our need, an offer came to pastor a church in another town several miles away. It seemed God had heard our prayers and brought the answer to us, rather than having us seek it out.

Bob talked with the church officers and learned that the church was in the same Baptist Association as the one that ordained him. There was a parsonage next door to the church where we would live, and the salary was one hundred twenty-five dollars per week. It seemed to be the answer to our problems, so Bob accepted their offer. But we didn't really seek God or ask our parents for godly counsel. It seemed so obvious—the timing, the parsonage, the salary. But now I know that circumstances and material provision don't automatically indicate God's choice, will, or blessing.

We decided to rent the house we had just built on Bob's family's land, and moved in to the parsonage during the Christmas Season. Our immediate need was to buy some furniture and appliances that we hadn't needed in our little apartment, mainly a kitchen table and chairs, a stove, and a washing machine and dryer.

We went to the Montgomery Ward store to look for the needed items. They had a special offer that day. You put your name in when you bought something and the winner's name would be drawn at a certain time. Just as we were about to leave the store, having bought the appliances we needed, the loudspeaker came on and we heard our names, "Bob and Darda Billester," saying that we had won a kitchen table and chair set. We were so excited because it was so unexpected, and it was something we really needed. We went home that night on flying feet, practically dancing into the house. When the kitchen set was delivered, it was beautiful—truly a gift from God. It was no cheap set. Rather it was very well made in the newer style of the day. It served us well for years.

We looked forward to our first Sunday services with some nervousness, for we knew no one at the church except the board members Bob had spoken with previously. Bob led the hymns then preached the sermon while I played the piano. I occasionally sang a solo, accompanied by Bob. I think a lady looked after Steve and Dale during the services. After church we went home, had lunch, and prepared for the evening service.

One morning I had a phone call from a church Elder who took care of the grounds. He informed me that I could not do laundry at certain times on certain days because he was watering the lawn.

My using the washing machine would deplete the flow of water to the lawns. I was surprised because babies in diapers need them washed frequently, and Dale was only a few months old. However, I told him I would do as he asked.

I am of the opinion that churches, and maybe other groups of people, have a corporate personality. If that is the case, this church group was quite different from our church in Loma Linda. That group had a warmer personality, while we learned as time went on, this one was cooler.

This church was somewhat legalistic, while Bob and I were more inter-denominational in our views. I don't remember any of the church people visiting us, or inviting us to their homes. When the women of the church had a gathering, I felt as if I was crashing the party. It was not easy to get into an ongoing conversation with them.

One particular Sunday morning has remained in my memory for all these years. It was the practice of churches to give their visitors a small token of thanks for visiting. Our church had pencils stamped with the church name. Before the sermon, Bob asked if there were any visitors in the audience. A few hands went up, so Bob asked the usher to give them pencils. The usher, now seated, said to Bob out loud, "Give out your own pencils" in a tone of voice that emphasized his response. I was speechless. I had been in lots of churches of various denominations, and never heard such a rude thing said. Another man did offer the pencils, which cleared the atmosphere so the rest of the service could continue as was expected. (Hmm. The Lord just reminded me I had not forgiven him. So I immediately did.)

I realize I have not been very positive in my memories of our time at this church, but my recollections are a blur of sameness. We had served there about a year and a half, when one night Bob came home to tell me we had been voted out of office. I thought we had been doing all right, but to learn essentially that we were fired with no previous warning, was devastating to each of us. I felt rejected and betrayed. I don't remember Bob voicing his feelings, but surely, he must have felt the same way. We remembered a former pastor who came to visit us soon after we moved in there.

He came to tell us that this church was known for being a "Pastor breaker." And so it proved.

The shock and pain we each felt went deep into our hearts and psyches, leaving scars that lasted for many years. It was our first serious rejection. For me, I felt that the way the church board handled the matter was uncaring, and I grieved for the treatment Bob received.

As I now look back and review that time, I realize we were not experienced enough for that type of church. We did not check to see if our doctrinal views and approach to ministry coincided with theirs. There are many types of Baptist churches and the denominational label says very little about the congregation's understanding of what it means to be a Christian and how to worship God. We did not do any research on this church, but took the word of others about it and accepted what was offered to us without question.

It was a very unpleasant experience, to say the least. We found out the hard way that we need to seek God's will in every matter, especially one where so many others are affected by our decisions. But, God being God, He was able to use the time of testing and trial to teach us new ways of depending on Him despite the disappointments and negatives during our time there. We had hoped to be a blessing to them, but we did not meet their requirements. It took many years until we could forgive them and be released, and our hearts be healed.

There's another factor in this experience that I now see in the perspective of years. Some churches are set in their own ways and they want to keep things the way they like them. We had a different understanding of what it means to live in relationship to Jesus, one that might have struck them as too loose, too broad, too uncomfortable. I don't know. It was an unhealthy atmosphere, and we were trying our best to serve as we understood the responsibilities to the flock our parents had exhibited. I think we would have kept trying in spite of the lack of connection with our congregation, but God released us abruptly so we were able to move on.

On a totally different note, when Dale was about 8 months old, he was able to crawl around the house. There was a screen door on the front door and Bob had put a latch on it high enough that Steve could not reach it. Steve was a smart and curious two-and-a-half-year-old. We had the front door open for any breezes to help cool our house. This one day I was busy in the kitchen. Thinking the screen door was latched I was not keeping an eye on the boys, but I heard the door bell ring. I went to see who was there, and I was absolutely shocked. I could not believe my eyes. A woman I did not know was holding Dale in her arms. She said she lived across the street and saw him crawling on the busy road! I thanked her profusely and took Dale in my arms and sat down breathless. Talk about God watching out for our little ones!

Bob, the boys, and I moved back to our house in El Monte. Our lot was fenced off from the rest of the Billester's property next door but a gate gave us easy access to each others home without having to go around by the street. It was so good to be in our own house. There was a nice-sized kitchen, a living room, and three bedrooms. Our bedroom in front was large, then there was a small one that would be Steve's room, and the back bedroom would be for Dale and the new child we were expecting in several months.

Bob was a very handy man who could fix most anything around the house. He was also a great mechanic who kept our cars running smoothly. That ability saved us quite a few dollars. As they grew, our boys learned those skills just from watching their father working.

We were settled in our home, but now what? Bob was out of a job. This was a time in our lives when we were not in ministry. Bob got a job delivering gravel, and I was once again a brand new mother. Bob and I proudly welcomed our third son, John Mark Billester, into our family.

Only days after John's birth, Michael told Bob that a small church in Monterey Park was looking for a pastor to fill in until they found a new one. Would Bob help them out? Thinking that it would be only a few weeks, he agreed.

After the morning service, one of the men asked Bob if I would attend the evening service, for they wanted to meet me. I did not want to go because John was too young to be out in public. But I thought I should, so I bundled John up in his blankets and went with Bob to see this church. Within days, the church called Bob and asked him to be their pastor. They liked his sermon and were happy to meet me, and thought we were the ones to lead their congregation.

Once more, our Sundays became very busy. Getting two little boys and a baby ready for church, as well as ourselves, was time consuming. We also had to plan ahead so that our lunch would be ready when we got home. Everyone would be hungry after Sunday School and morning service. I usually put a small roast in the oven to cook while we were gone.

When we got home, I finished the rest of the meal. While I was doing that, Bob would go next door to his parent's to talk about the morning service. We didn't know how long he would be gone, so we waited for him. That was aggravating to me. At times I wanted to ask him to visit his parents after we ate lunch but I didn't say anything, partly because both of our family patterns were similar. My father Percy, and Bob's father Michael, were both missionaries who would be gone for many weeks. We didn't know how long they would be gone, so we waited to welcome them home. Our waiting for Bob was just a tiny example of that. I think that I may have gone ahead at times and fed the boys while we waited. In those days, the 1950s, the husband was head of the household, and generally what he said or did, was agreed to.

As we grew into the ministry there, we found that the people were kind and friendly and they welcomed us. As the weeks went by we were more comfortable in the work. The congregation began to grow, and some younger couples joined us with their children.

After a few months we started a choir. One of the new members was a gift from God. She was a music teacher in the local schools. Margaret began playing the organ, while I played the piano or led the choir on Sunday mornings. Our choir, though small, came together well. We developed to the point that we could present a Cantata one evening during the Christmas seasons.

In the late fall, Bob was let go from his job driving the gravel truck. Now we did not have enough income for our family, and Bob did not find any jobs available for truck drivers. After thinking about it and talking together, I said I would get a job for the Christmas holidays, and then in January maybe jobs for him would open up. Thus began my working career, although I didn't know this job would be the beginning of many years in the work force. My job meant that Bob could concentrate on his ministry. He didn't need to be at the church every day, so he could help out with some of the things that had to be done at home as well as keeping an eye on Steve and Dale.

Once I got used to the new daily routine, I felt as if I led three lives—as a wife and mother, the church musician, and a store cashier. Even though almost every hour was taken, it did prove to be God's plan for me, and I knew that He would give me the strength day by day, wherever I was. I sometimes said that I put on my high heels at 7 a.m. and took them off at 11:00 p.m. Eventually I got a job at Avery Label Company, a place that made adhesive labels, and I found the work stimulating, interesting, and fulfilling. I worked there 28 years.

By this time, Steve was about 5 years old. He was curious about many things, and would go over often to his grandma Amanda's office to see what she was doing. She took care of the business part of the mission society. She began teaching him to read and to file record cards alphabetically. He told me recently that when he went to kindergarten he read the stories to other children. Then he added that doing the filing under her oversight brought out his enjoyment of data management that he still uses in his work today.

One Wednesday night, I came home from work to find that Bob had already started getting dinner ready, as he sometimes did. We had a meeting at the church and hurried through the meal. Bob told me that he felt he should stay home from the meeting that night instead of asking his mother to stay with the boys. I thought that was odd, but didn't ask him why. That was the day John decided to climb a power pole outside, slipped, and was impaled by a protruding spike under his right arm. I wrote about that night of perfectly placed persons, from Steve and Dale, to Bob's unusual time at home, to the specialist in vein surgery that reattached John's severed vessels. Whoever heard of a specialist practicing at a small town hospital, let alone in an Industrial Medical Clinic? Only God could have set up the perfect scenario to have the right people in the right place at the right time!

Whenever we could, we used our vacation time to visit my family in Victoria, B.C. Bob did most of the driving, we took the ferry, and the boys got more and more excited because they knew when the ferry docked, it was only a half hour to Nana and Bumpa's house.

Dad always had some fun things for our boys to do with their cousins. A favorite place was Smuggler's Cove, a beach only a few miles away. It was a lovely sandy beach with driftwood to sit on or play with, as well as a great swimming hole. Bob took the opportunity to go fishing with a friend, which he loved to do. Sometimes they brought supper home, having caught some nice-sized salmon.

As the 1960s came to a close, our boys were growing up. They were strong, sturdy like their father, and active. Steve loved science like me, Dale and John loved baseball, and all of them were musically gifted. Steve graduated with honors from high school in 1969. Several universities wrote letters to him inviting him to continue his education at their campuses. However, California Institute of Technology (Cal Tech) offered him a scholarship. That was a gift from the Lord because we would not have been able to pay their fees. It was a wonderful opportunity to learn the subjects he was interested in at a school dedicated to those areas of knowledge.

When Steve learned that Cal Tech offered flying lessons leading to a pilot's license, he signed up. He chose one of the instructors and started flight training. He was even able to sign Bob up for the same training, and Bob also began lessons. He loved it, and loved sharing that activity with his son. The training in the planes took place at our El Monte Airport, right in our backyard, so to speak. Steve earned his pilot's license. His delight in flying has lasted throughout his lifetime. He even purchased his own plane.

Even before starting high school, John was playing the drums for a quartet named The Crownsmen, formed by our neighbor. They traveled around to various churches in the Los Angeles basin, continuing throughout his high school and early college days. They branched out to do summer tours, and on one, the air conditioning unit in their bus broke down. John sent me his memories of that special day, which I will add here:

"The weather was very hot, humid and sticky. We found a mechanic shop who could do the repair work, so our travel schedule was halted for several hours. The heat and humidity made it way too uncomfortable to be inside the bus, so some of us decided to find a spot outside and write letters home.

"With letters in hand we asked for directions to the closest post office so we could mail them. Off we went wearing shorts and shoes but no shirts. As I recall the post office was quite some distance away but with nothing else to do, we set out on our trek.

"We found the post office, mailed our letters and it was on our return trip that things took a turn for the worse. It was late afternoon and traffic was heavy on a main thoroughfare with two lanes running in either direction. We were walking well off the road on the gravel shoulder moving in the direction of the traffic.

"At one point I heard a vehicle on gravel accelerating quickly from behind us. I turned and looked just in time to see an older white Ford van that was passing traffic on the right and coming straight for me. I had only enough time to raise my right arm and elbow to protect the right side of my head and lifted my right leg and knee to prepare for the impact—BAM!

"The impact threw me forward 15 to 20 feet. I remember rolling several times but ultimately rising up to an upright standing position. I was obviously stunned along with those who were walking with me. The van stopped and I remember the windshield was broken and the right side mirror was broken off and just hanging on the side of the van.

"The van suddenly took off without checking on me or leaving any information. Law enforcement was called and responded right away. I was transported to the hospital for a medical check and the only things they discovered was a few pieces of gravel were embedded in my lower back. Once they were removed I was released with no broken bones or further necessity for future medical attention. What a miracle!

"I remember being on the bus later that evening. The air conditioning had been repaired and we were rolling down the highway as usual. I was on my knees praying at my bunk, thanking the Lord for sparing my life. My eyes were full of tears, knowing He could have taken me Home that day so very quickly. I knew that He still had plans for me and wanted to use me for His glory in the future. And, this was not the first time in my short 17 years of life that He could have taken me Home.

"I was obviously very sore the next few days, but I was still able to play the drums as our tour continued without 'missing a beat.'"

When John called me to let me know about it, he started the conversation something like this, "Hi, Mom. I don't want you to worry or be afraid, or anything, but…" I was so struck by his story, and Bob and I were also so thankful to the Lord for His protective hand on John, for we had been praying for the gang on this trip out of state.

For some while, Bob had been feeling depressed and discouraged with his ministry. I don't know the cause, but there were some Sunday mornings when he would sit on the edge of the bed and say in a sad tone, "I wish I didn't have to go to church." Then he would slowly get up and start getting ready for the day.

After hearing this and realizing his need for the Lord's help, I suggested to him that he take some time off and go some place where he could have privacy and seek the Lord to give him a new call to the ministry.

We heard that Kathryn Kuhlman, known as a Faith Healer, although she disavowed that name, was holding monthly meetings on Sunday afternoons at the Shrine Auditorium in Los Angeles.

We decided to go to the next meeting, so that Sunday we left church immediately after we closed the service and headed for L.A. The service started with prayer and singing. Ushers moved up and down the aisles looking for empty seats for those still coming in.

Kathryn began preaching her sermon to a point where the Holy Spirit started telling her where healings were happening. She would announce that someone in a certain area was being healed of certain illnesses such as heart problems, or arthritis, or deafness. This continued for a while almost without stopping. She asked that those who were healed would raise their hands, and an usher would tell that person to walk forward to the platform.

One by one, they approached Kathryn and told her what they were healed from. Her interest in them was loving and she would praise God for them. She had them demonstrate their healing and then pray a blessing over them. She frequently said that she did not know why God healed some and not others. She was insistent that the Holy Spirit did the healing, she was only the vessel to give the message.

We sat and were awed by what we saw from our vantage point in the balcony. As we joined the people leaving after the service was over, Bob remarked that that woman had more power of God in her little finger than he did in his big body.

We kept going to those meetings for several months, and since Bob was a pastor, he was able to get a seat on the platform with other pastors. He saw crippled individuals walking out of their wheelchairs, or giving up their crutches. Some who had back problems were able to bend over without pain. Others who were healed of serious diseases were cautioned to go back to their doctors and get tested to prove to the doctors that they were healed.

From Bob's seat on the platform, he was in awe from what he saw close up. He could see Kathryn Kuhlman at prayer standing in the wings. She prayed until the Holy Spirit filled her to the point that her visage changed. She would not come on stage until He was fully in charge and she was not.

Some that were healed were Christians and many were not. To them, she would say with a big smile, "God love ya", place her hand on them and bless them. When she did that, the person often fell to the floor in the power of the Holy Spirit.

We continued to attend her services until it was impossible for us to make it in time to get seated. People chartered buses to bring them to L.A., and others lined up in front of the doors for 2 or more hours just to get a seat.

One day, a little later, Bob said to me that he was going to go down to the church every evening and pray to God for His help until God did something for him. On the fourth evening he came home a changed man. The Holy Spirit had filled him with His love and power while he was at the church, and the relief, joy, and love of God was evident on his face. The people at the church noticed the change and Bob told them what had happened, and that the same Holy Spirit was eager to fill every one of them.

The whole atmosphere in the services was different. Bob's sermons were different—the Spirit of the Lord was there. Some of the members asked for the baptism in the Holy Spirit, and others were becoming aware of their need for it. A few of the young women received the Holy Spirit and began witnessing to students at the local high school about the goodness of God.

The church also began going to the Union Rescue Mission on Skid Row in L.A. every month. Bob preached, and sometimes I sang a solo. We were blessed when we saw men come forward to ask the Lord to be their Savior. On a few occasions Bob was asked to preach on their morning radio program.

Things went smoothly for about six months, when a new couple joined our church. They became quite friendly with one of the board members and his wife who were considering this step to receive the Holy Spirit. They decided to spend a weekend together. Whatever the influence the new couple had, they turned the thinking of the board member and wife to believe the filling of the Holy Spirit was not for this time.

From that weekend on, a church split was in the making. Bob and I did not realize it until one of our trusted members told us what some of the members were doing. Not one of them came to Bob to talk to him about their problem with this teaching. They began to bring discord into the church to get Bob out.

Their tactics then were much the same as we see happening in our government today. One side worked quietly together to keep us from knowing what was really going on, and making contacts with previous people who were no longer members to come to the meeting and vote with them. We could not do the same, as it was against the church By-Laws.

Bob and I were very concerned for the church and did much praying and seeking God for His plan, whether or not it was our time to move on to another church. God gave us a real peace and confidence that whichever way the final vote went, we were all right. God had the whole thing in His hands.

We did not tell the boys what was going on because we did not want them to look with disfavor on those who were against us, because they knew them, too. They knew something was not right, but did not know details.

One way that showed us that God was for us, was when two of the men who were working against the filling of the Spirit went to the minister of the church where Bob was ordained to ask his help in their pursuit for the church. He asked them if they had talked to Bob about their concerns. They admitted they had not. When he heard that, he told them that he could not do anything to help them. If they had talked to Bob and then come to him, he could have stepped in to counsel Bob. But since they did not, he was unable to do anything at all to help them.

A business meeting of the church membership was announced and a Vote of Confidence in the pastor would be taken. That night, we left the boys at home and Bob and I went to the church. We knew what to expect because we had been in that position before, and it was not fun.

When we arrived, Bob went to the front seat and I sat in the back alone. My heart was heavy with grief for what Bob would have to sit through, yet I was still confident that God held this meeting in His hands. I was praying for God's presence to be in the meeting.

When the meeting was called to order, the people for Bob spoke and said how much he had done for the church. Then the opposition spoke and said that he had failed in bringing this new teaching into the church. It was against our church doctrinal statement. I think they gave Bob a chance to speak, but I don't remember. Then came the time to take the vote of confidence in his ministry.

When it was finally counted, we won the vote to remain at the church. The deacon in charge of the meeting called for a second vote, thinking there must have been an error. The second vote was the same as the first. As a result, we lost half the congregation. I'm sure as we left that night, they did not expect our church to last for any length of time.

On the contrary, our church did not fail. Bob said he would give up his salary for six months. People gave as they could for some of them were on a fixed income. But as time went on and the funds came in I felt like God "kited" some of the checks, because we were able to continue paying the church bills. Bob's salary was then reinstated.

More important was the atmospheric change in the church. There was such a sense of the Lord's presence, and love flowed among the members in a way that had not been there before. The services were full of praise and prayer to the extent that at times Bob did not preach so the honor to the Lord would not be broken. The services would end and then we stood outside for another 45 minutes or so, just talking about what the Lord was doing in our lives.

One thing that happened to me at that time was the Lord began giving me what I called Writings, for want of a better word. He would give me a few words in my mind, and when I wrote them down a continuing flow of words came until the page was filled or the subject completed. This blessing continued for many years and I decided to share them with family, friends, and some church members who would appreciate the encouraging words God gave us all. The Holy Spirit still gives me writings from time to time, and I still share them when He leads me to do so.

Wonderfully, sovereignly, the Lord started doing some miracles in our services. One lady was healed of a blood disease. Another person was freed from constant headaches. One of the young women whom I am still in contact with, told me her story recently in an email.

After one of our meetings at the Union Rescue Mission she was driving home on the I-5 freeway that evening. All of a sudden her car started stuttering and losing acceleration, and she knew she was going to stop in the middle of the fast lane. She could not move over to slower lanes. She immediately prayed that the Lord would not let anyone be hurt or killed in the cars behind her. Then she saw a small red foreign convertible pull up behind her and stop. She prayed that the driver would not be hit either. He stayed behind her while she kept trying to start the car.

Her car finally started and she cautiously began to move over lane by lane to the side of the freeway. A truck was parked there and she knew he was checking on her. The driver of the red car spoke to that driver, then came back and told my friend that the Highway Patrol had been called. She looked up to thank him for his help but he and the car had disappeared. She never had a chance to thank him, and wondered if he had been one of God's angels sent to protect her in such a dangerous situation.

In the church, God was still doing His work to provide things that were needed. One of the great needs was for new pews. The old wooden ones were getting hard to sit on and were uncomfortable. Our congregation began praying about it for God to provide the funding.

Around that time, the City of Monterey Park sent a representative to Bob to let us know they were going to widen the street on which the church was located. They would take a certain footage in width from the length of church property and pay us for it. What an answer to our prayers!

Bob and a couple of men on the board started looking for new pews to see what was available in our price range. One company had just what we wanted, and so we ordered as many as would fill our auditorium. They were made of oak wood with a light blue cushioning. When they were delivered, it was so good to just look at them and then find that they were so comfortable to sit on. We gave much praise to God for His working on our behalf.

The next thing God had to do was to point us to a church that could use our old pews as a gift. Once again, God showed His hand. One day Bob got a phone call from a pastor in San Fernando Valley, quite a distance from our church. Their church was praying, "Lord, somewhere in Los Angeles, you have the pews we need." Bob assured the pastor that our pews were his for their church.

After the exchange had been made, our church was invited to visit them for their celebration and thanksgiving for God's provision and answered prayer. Both churches were rejoicing in this evidence of God's goodness.

In the fall of 1969, Mother and Dad invited us to join them for Christmas. We had not been able to do that before, because it is such a busy time for a church. But we decided we would spend Christmas with them rather than our usual August vacation. Bob arranged for Michael to preach on the Sundays we were gone, and I took my vacation time.

Steve was a freshman at Cal Tech and wanted to get a Christmas job earning some money for school, since all freshmen had to live in the dormitories. He knew our funds were short, and he wanted to do all he could to keep the additional burden off of us. We told him we appreciated his desire, but we wanted him to come with us because it would probably be the last family trip we would make.

On Friday night, we were getting ready to leave when Bob's grandmother came over. She was very concerned about us starting so late when we were so tired. Bob listened to her, then said he just felt strongly that we should leave that night and not wait until morning. She again spoke her concerns, and Bob thanked her, but said we would leave that night.

It's a good thing we did, although we wouldn't know the reason until the next morning. By then we had crossed the Ridge Route, the steep high road through the mountains north of Los Angeles, and were well on our way. We were all awake listening to the car radio when we learned that a sudden snow storm had closed the Ridge Route just after midnight. Had we waited, we would not have been able to make our trip because it is the main route north on the I-5 freeway.

Once again, we crossed the border and arrived at the port for the ferry ride to Vancouver Island and Victoria, which was all dressed up in its Christmas finery. Mother and Dad had the house all nicely decorated. We spent a wonderful Christmas with my parents and they enjoyed the time with our boys, who were reaching adulthood. We did not know our boys would never see Nana alive again.

IN THE VALLEY OF THE SHADOW

New Year's Day, January 1, 1970, began a decade of important events for our family—events of happiness and others full of sorrows. Almost every year of that decade had some major event that resulted in quite a few changes in our families.

My parents had taken a tour to Hawaii to give Mother some rest from helping to take care of her mother who lived in Abbotsford, B.C., some forty miles east of Vancouver. One of the people who was on that tour was a woman who went even though she had the flu. Mother was exposed to that flu and contracted it. Not only that, but the day they got home they got news that Grandma had passed away. So Mother and Dad traveled to Abbotsford to attend to her mother's funeral and other related matters. That grievous loss, plus the flu she caught from the woman, caused my mother to be very ill. When they got home Mother went to see the doctor, but her regular physician was on vacation. The substitute doctor did not check her properly and she developed a serious case of pneumonia. That caused her heart to weaken, and she had to spend time in the hospital before she could come home.

Dad resigned from the SCA and other things he was engaged in so that he could fully care for Mother. She was practically bed-ridden, and on a special diet to keep her heart from developing further problems.

I could not go to see her because I was still working, but I kept in touch by phone and I was able to talk with her occasionally. I let them know we were all praying for her. It was so hard for me to not be there to help, knowing how weak she was and how my Dad was so involved in her ongoing care. He was concerned for her well-being and diligent to do all he could for her, but it troubled his heart and I wanted so much to help share the load.

The next year, Dale graduated from high school. He tried a few jobs, but nothing fit him. One day he went to visit our neighbor's locksmith business. After talking to our neighbor, he decided to give it a try. Dale seemed to have all the right aptitudes for that work, and he learned all he could of the intricacies of that service.

Meanwhile, Dale heard of a musical group called "Rudy and the Chosen Ones" that traveled to give concerts at churches. He joined them for the experience that belonging to a musical group would give him. One member was a young lady named Elizabeth, who caught his eye. They became friends, and he learned that she lived in another suburb not far away. Their friendship deepened and he proposed to her. I knew deep in my heart that they would marry, so I was not surprised when they got engaged. Bob talked with him about getting married so young, but we did not deter him from doing so.

On a particular day in John's junior year, he was walking to a Spanish class with a sophomore named Caprice. The Sadie Hawkin's Dance was going to be held in a week or so. The students called this the "Backwards Dance" because the girls got to ask the boys for a date. Gathering up her courage, Caprice asked John if he would take her to the dance. He said he would.

Over the months, their friendship grew as they shared their interests with each other. Caprice went with a friend to a couple of John's baseball games and cheered with the others when he hit two home runs. John invited her to go to the high school to hear his group play. Caprice said it was fun to watch him playing the drums. She was a new Christian and loved to hear the songs about Jesus.

During the early months of 1972, Mother was not doing very well. There was no improvement in her condition and she seemed very tired. In late March, my phone rang and Dad said that Mother was failing and I should come to see her. I arranged time off and booked a flight to Victoria. Dad picked me up at the airport and took me immediately to the hospital. I was shocked to see how very thin she was. Her features were so sharp and her bones were really prominent. She was in a coma, I think, as she made no response to my greeting. I stayed with Dad for a few days, and then flew home.

Ten days later Dad called me to tell me that Mother had died and her funeral was planned for that weekend. The funeral parlor was packed with people who knew and loved her, and all our family who could travel. Many of those who had been with us on Belmont Avenue were there. Many spoke of Mother's hospitality and goodness, and there were telegrams read with memories of Mother's impact on them during her lifetime.

After I returned home, I kept in touch with Dad by telephone. Before Mother died, his voice on the phone always had a lilt to it. Now when I talked with him, his voice was flat with his grieving. It was so devastating to him, but I could tell he was truly trusting the Lord to walk with him and comfort him in the days following her death.

Our church was still enjoying the presence of the Lord in our services. Once more we had a fairly good number of attendees who really loved the Lord. Bob's salary had been restored and we were able to turn part of the offerings to other missionary works.

The rest of the year passed smoothly and the Christmas season was fast approaching. Bob and I went Christmas shopping after dinner one night. When we returned, one of the boys met us at the car to let us know that Grandma Barr had just passed away. That was a complete surprise and hard to believe. Her birthday was just a few days away and she would have been 103 years old.

Juxtaposed with these sorrows was the start of a new beginning. Dale and Elizabeth were getting married. Bob officiated at the ceremony, talking about the responsibilities of marriage, and what God had intended when He ordained that a man would leave father and mother and cleave to his wife. The vows then were spoken, the rings exchanged, and the young couple began their new life together as husband and wife.

Only a couple of months later, Bob said he was having trouble with a sore on his tongue. His doctor looked at it and thought it was just a type of canker sore. After his second visit with the same diagnosis, we decided to go to another doctor for a second opinion because we didn't think it looked good.

That doctor took a careful look at it from several angles, and told Bob that he thought it could be cancer. He referred us to a very good Face and Neck Specialist. We were shocked and fearful with this diagnosis. Bob wasn't that old, we thought, and wondered what caused this odd sore in his mouth. The specialist looked at it and tested it very carefully. He confirmed the cancer diagnosis, and promptly set up a date for surgery a short time later.

We called on our friends and family for prayer, and let the church know Bob would not be preaching for awhile. They also joined our prayer team which kept us above the fear of what might happen. I phoned Dad to let him know our bad news. He spoke to me, though I don't remember what he said. But whatever it was it would have been kind, comforting, with a great deal of godly wisdom and knowledge with a tenderness that also encouraged.

The surgery went very well, and Bob was out of the hospital within days. He felt well and his speech was not affected very much, so he was back in the pulpit a week or so later. He was given a choice between chemotherapy and radiation treatments. He chose radiation as being less dreadful than the chemotherapy. After he had completed his radiation therapy, he had frequent checkup appointments that were quite encouraging, and we continued life with some hope that he would really come through this difficult time.

I kept up with Dad by frequent phone calls. The flat tone of his voice was still the same, although it was calm and welcoming when we talked. He told me that he was going to Toronto to be interviewed by Douglas C. Percy, who was writing a book about the Shantymen's ministry. While there, he wanted to visit the mission headquarters and see some old friends he hadn't seen for quite a long time. I wished him well on this trip and thought it would be good for him to have a change of scenery and purpose.

One day in early 1974, my brother Frank phoned me and said, "Sis! You'll never guess what just happened!" His voice was charged with excitement.

"What happened, Frank?" I asked curiously.

"Dad's getting married!" he said.

My jaw dropped. I was thunderstruck! I had never known that Dad was interested in another woman or even considered the fact that he might remarry. Had I thought about it, I would have realized that Percy's loving nature had to have someone with whom to share that love.

I knew Dad had gone to meet some old friends while he was in Toronto. This lady, Vera Coulter McPherson, was one of the four Coulter girls whom Dad and Mother knew from the early days of their ministry. They had maintained contact through all the years and visited together whenever the occasion arose. She, too, had lost her spouse.

Vera was a perfect partner for Dad. She had the same spirit of hospitality that he had. Her husband was a pastor for many years, so she was used to sharing her husband's time with his parishioners. Also, her long-term friendship with Dad and Mother gave them each great insights about the other one.

They were married in Toronto, and I was able to attend the wedding along with other family members from out of town. God had indeed brought them together. Once again I could hear the lilt in my father's voice when I phoned him. They suited each other so well and were happy together for the sixteen years given to them.

The first of January, 1975, began what I call "My watershed year." It was a year of trial and testing that none of us could expect, or dream about. On December 31, 1975, the only thing the same was most of our family was still together, and I was still working at Avery.

John and Caprice were happily planning their wedding for the end of June, and looking forward to Bob marrying them as he had done for Dale and Elizabeth. But Bob's cancer returned under his tongue and surgery was not possible. He was asked to take one more week of radiation. It had some very serious side effects. I came home on my lunch hours to help him and prepare his food.

At the same time, Bob's mother Amanda was showing signs of Dementia and her health was failing. Toward the end of March, she passed into the presence of Jesus. Michael was distraught but grieved silently, as did all the rest of us. She was buried in the section of Forrest Lawn named "The Court of Freedom."

Bob continued to decline and on the evening of May 6th, he experienced some severe pain, and I called the family to let them know. They had just arrived when the ambulance came. As the medics were getting Bob on the gurney, I saw him slump, and knew that he had passed into the Lord's presence. He was only 49 years old. We all had another grief to add to our hearts so soon.

Stephen, Michael and I followed the ambulance to the hospital, and waited there until the doctor came and confirmed his death. It was strange looking at Bob and not seeing any life in him. You knew he wasn't sleeping.

We came home, Michael to his empty house, and Steve and I to mine. I remember sitting on Steve's bed side by side and talking about what had happened. He was very quiet, and I think I was unloading some of my grief as my dear son listened.

I was bewildered. We had prayed—fervently. The church people and our family had been believing God would heal him. But He didn't. We believed in miracles of healing. Bob and I had seen many at the Kuhlman meetings. What happened? Kathryn herself had said she didn't know why God healed some and not others. Well-meaning people say a lot of things to try to help with the pain of the grief. But we were devastated. "He's in a better place" just wasn't that much help. Yes, God is sovereign. It's even possible that, in the sweet old by and by, we will know the answer to our question "Why?" But all I knew was we had asked and He had said, "No."

Someone said, "God has three answers to prayer, 'Yes,' 'Not yet,' and, 'I have something better.'" Someone else said, "God's will is what we would choose if we knew all the facts." I suppose the most important thing is not to decide God doesn't care or isn't really there. Throughout my long years, I have seen too much evidence that He does care, even when we can't see how, and He is truly there, walking with us every step of the difficult way— though it means a broken heart, an empty place, and a slow walk through the Valley of the Shadow of Death.

Steve's friend, Herschel Carlson, officiated at Bob's funeral. Many of our church members, my boss, and a few other friends from work attended, which I appreciated so much. He was buried near his mom in the Billester family plot in the Court of Freedom section. Even after all these years since then, the name "Court of Freedom" is a description of a spiritual reality, and still gives me a lift to my spirit.

During my grieving, and for a long time afterward, I felt like I had lost half of myself. I guess I really had since we had such a good marriage in supporting and complementing each other's strong and weak points. Sometimes when we went to minister to someone, Bob would say something and then I would get something to add to it, and so on. We were a team. We moved as one sharing the love of Jesus with a troubled, hurting person in need. I also felt like there was a huge hole in my heart.

In one stroke, my husband, my best friend, my confidante, and my pastor, was taken from me. Who could I talk to? I think everyone in the family felt the same way. I was also concerned about Michael, who had lost his wife of many years and his only son.

John and Caprice were willing to postpone their wedding, but we agreed Bob would not want them to wait. Their wedding was as happy an event as could be with hearts fluctuating between tears of sorrow and tears of joy. Steve's friend Herschel took Bob's place officiating at the ceremony. Maybe the vows had a little more meaning at their wedding because of the sorrow in our hearts.

Michael, Steve, Dale, Elizabeth and I began wondering what do we do now? Our spiritual adviser, Bob, was not available. Who do we go to for advice? How can our family stick together? We were leaning on each other for whatever the future held.

A couple of years earlier God had started giving me Writings to speak to me in my times of need. This one is from 1989. Even though it was not given during Bob's time of death, the content describes how we felt, and, as I wrote about this painful time in our lives, I felt the Holy Spirit nudge me to share it with you here.

"When the Lord fed the 5,000, after they were all filled, the disciples gathered up the fragments from the meal (the leftovers) and they filled 12 baskets.

"About the fragments—broken pieces—they contained the same nutrient value as what had been consumed. They were potentially as valuable but—they were not used then.

"We are not told how they were used but presumably the Lord and His disciples were fed from them, since God does not waste things. The broken pieces were all gathered up. They were not left behind, or discarded.

"Sometimes we feel like a leftover—a broken piece. But the Lord declares our value to Him, and He will gather us up, too."

I think we all felt like "broken pieces," and wondered what to do. How could we come together as a new kind of family under these circumstances?

I went back to work, as did the others, but it was hard, and occasionally I had to go to the Ladies Restroom where there was a separate room with a couch. I went in there to give release to my tears that came unexpectedly. When I had cried myself out, I went back to my office with red eyes. My work companions understood, and were very kind to me.

Bob and I had promised Michael and Amanda when the time came that they needed help, we would take care of them. Now that there was just Michael and me of the four, I would take Michael to live with me, wherever that was. We knew we could not simply move into my house or his, selling the other property where we had lived so many happy years with our beloved spouse. We needed a different arrangement, but one that would make it possible for all of us to stay together.

The five of us got together one day to talk this matter over and see what we could come up with. We were also praying that God would lead us and provide the right property(ies) that would be suitable. As we talked, each one of us mentioned some particular thing we would like to have in the new place.

Dale and Elizabeth started looking and Elizabeth's mother, Norma, who was a Real Estate Agent, also looked over places that were available and suitable for our needs. What they found was a compound on a big piece of property in Fontana, with three separate houses on it. It was beautiful, and it seemed perfect.

The story of God's provision is long and detailed, so I'll tell you only that it was a huge thing for me to be making such a momentous decision with no one knowing the full story except God. After I saw the property Dale and Elizabeth had found, I went home in a swarm of thoughts. My heart was screaming to the Lord—"What do You want me to do? What should I do? Is this God's will for me/us? How will I know? How will I pay for it? Can I do this? Is there anything better on the market?"

Prayer was not far from my thoughts.

The following Wednesday evening Dale, Elizabeth and I went to take another look with Norma as our guide. She explained the pros and cons of this place to us, and asked me what did I want to do. I finally realized that God would not sign the sales document for me. I had to do that. And so with a thumping heart, I wrote my name on the document on condition that my house sell within 60 days.

The very next day Norma called me to say that a couple had spoken to the seller and offered him cash for the property. However, because I had signed the document, the seller was tied up with me for at least 60 days. God was timing this matter.

I was so fearful of this step requiring more faith than I had. When I was home from work I was on my knees quite frequently begging God to help me. God would give me peace at those times. Then Norma would tell me that the couple was calling the seller almost daily to see if I had defaulted. Back I would go to my knees pleading for God's peace. This went on for some time.

Finally, in desperation, I said, "God, you say I am not to be fearful, but I am. Please show me how to be at peace and unafraid." Suddenly, I had a mental picture of me and Jesus at some kind of crossroad with direction signs. It was like God was pointing the way I should go by myself. But then He let me know that He would be with me every step of the way, and I would be victorious in this matter. That gave me the peace I sorely needed and I got up from my knees and could smile and praise God at last.

Moving day, December 4, 1975, came quickly and I was up early to be ready for the moving truck. They packed everything and took off for Fontana, with me following them. We drove down the long driveway into this huge property which was now mine and parked outside the second house, the one Michael and I would live in.

This may seem strange to you, but to me, the fact that all my furniture fit in the right places in the new house, even the pictures, was a sign that God meant me/us to be there.

Elizabeth and Dale moved into the main house, and Steve moved in to the third house about that same time. So we were now in a family enclave that God had prearranged for us to have that met our needs so well.

Each one of us found the things we had said earlier that we really wanted in our homes. I wanted an entry hall so that a person at the door didn't just step in from the porch. My house had that entry hall. Dale and Elizabeth wanted a separate dining room because they had that furniture. The main house had that dining room. It also had three bedrooms so that when guests came to visit, there was a place for them. Steve had mentioned that a swimming pool might be nice. Well, it wasn't in his house, but there was a nice one about 12 feet deep, on the property. All of this seemed to be another sign from the Lord as to His purpose for us in this specific place.

With the house came the right to have a regular run of irrigation water. When I inquired about it, I found I could have the minimum of a four hour run of water every other Saturday. That's what the pool was for. All the piping and equipment necessary for receiving the water was already in place.

It was a nice thought to dream of splashing about in the deep water in the pool on a hot California summer day. That playfulness was only a sideline of having the pool. It's main purpose was to hold irrigation water to feed the fruit trees on the property, and there were several big trees.

In order for the water to reach the thirsty trees planted on sandy soil, we had to dig a long ditch from the pool to the trees. At least the sandy soil made the digging go faster. They had to be completely ready because when 8:00 a.m. came on that Saturday morning and I pushed the button that opened the flood gate for the water, it immediately came gushing out, filling the pool as well as sending the water racing down the ditch.

From watching the water running down the ditch, I learned a couple of spiritual lessons. One was that God wants us to know that we need, and prepare ourselves for, the filling of His Holy Spirit. Are we digging away from our hearts things that are not honoring to God so that we can be ready to receive from His heart the gifts He wants to give us? Another little lesson was that any weeds on the edge of the ditch would cause a little eddy there, and the water was kept from reaching the trees. Do we have little sins that seem to have little impact on our spiritual growth, but actually keep us from growing closer to God and being watered by His Word?

As I write this book, I am seeing things about my life I would not have known except for the long, backward look over the richness of years. Recently I spent time praying, asking the Lord for insights so I could better understand myself and the way He has been guiding and carefully shaping me as a skilled and careful potter lovingly bringing into being the person He designed me to be. This is what He showed me:

I have lived my life within a closed circle under someone's authority. First my family, then with the Billesters. I did have jobs, but came home to the family as a daughter. Until Bob died I had never lived alone as a single person. Even then I had Michael with me.

Purchasing Fontana was my first experience of having to make decisions on my own authority and without adequate counsel except from God. It was a very difficult situation lasting several months. But God brought me through it to victory. That was a freeing experience for me. I did not know until then how to exert the authority I had in my physical life. Same in my spiritual life. In the years to come, I would need to be able to use both—in decision-making for even bigger needs, and in prayer as the families grew and the world began to sink into increasing darkness. I didn't know that at the time, of course; I was too busy trying to get through each day and each new thing. For now, anyway, we were settled. And we were together.

STARTING A NEW WAY OF LIFE

Now we were all settled in our new residences, and enjoying the largeness of the property. We felt we could stand and stretch our arms as wide as possible and touch nothing. We were in a neighborhood with lots of homes, but our property was totally surrounded by a beautifully-built wide stone wall, about four feet high.

We resumed our old way of life in a brand new setting. We still had to drive to work, only a longer distance. Household chores were the same, but in new houses. There were new grocery stores, new doctor's offices, etc., all requiring an adjustment in our schedules.

Christmas was just a couple of weeks away and we looked forward to our first celebration in this new setting. Together we opened our gifts and shared a very good Christmas dinner. Our hearts were full of praise that we had been brought through the extremely difficult months from the old life to this new one.

I was glad to have Michael living with me. We were company for each other in our progress through our grief and huge changes in life. Since Michael had been gone so much on his missionary work, I did not know him that well. It was a learning experience for us to get used to each other's habits. It did not take long, and life settled in to a good routine for the next several years.

In early 1977, John went to the Police Academy for training. Not long after, he graduated from the police academy. He gave the Valedictorian speech about their training and the police officers who had trained them. It was a very good talk and we were all so proud of him. Other good things blessed our family soon after. John and Caprice welcomed my first granddaughter, Shannon, and Dale and Elizabeth welcomed my first grandson, Jason, into our family.

I found a good church in a nearby community, where the pastor preached from the Word of God every Sunday. It was so good to hear the Scripture meanings opened up to our understanding. They had a good choir so I joined that as a place where I could use my musical talents.

A few years had passed since Bob died, and I began wondering about marrying again. Who would it be, and where could I meet him? A friend told me about a Singles Group, and suggested that

I attend their meeting and see what it was like. She gave me the address and meeting schedule.

On the next meeting date I drove to the place. Quite a few people were there. I believe there were more women than men. I introduced myself and chatted with a few of them to get a feel if this was a good thing for me. Then I went home and thought I would go again.

At the next meeting, a gentleman came up to talk with me. We had a short conversation, and I began to feel like I had a sign on my chest that said "Available." I thought, "What if I like this guy and we start dating?" It scared me. I realized I was certainly not ready to remarry, so I never went back.

What I did do was turn to the Lord Who had a plan for my life. I said if He had a husband for me, that was fine, but I wasn't going to look for one. If He did not intend me to marry again, that was fine, too. I had a good job, I didn't feel the need for a male companion, and I still had Michael in my home. I left it in His hands, and ceased being concerned about the "If's" of the matter. I knew His plan would be His best for me whichever way it turned out.

The following summer Steve wanted to take a trip flying his own plane and he invited me to go along. I quickly said I would go with him. Michael would be fine at home with Dale and Elizabeth right next door.

Steve's plane was a small two-seater side by side. On the appointed day, Steve went around the plane checking everything that should be checked before takeoff. He had told me about weight restrictions and had made sure I had complied. Steve looked all around us to make sure everything was clear, and we started rolling down the runway until the plane left the earth.

The day was beautiful as we watched the scenery below us get smaller and smaller. Steve gave me the flight maps to read when he needed the information. It was interesting to see the usual cities going north but in a different configuration on the maps.

At one point we had to take an alternative route because of a windstorm in our path. Steve did that, filing the new flight plan as required. Then he called ahead and made reservation so we'd have a place to stay when we landed in Redmond, OR. The next morning we headed toward Seattle, arriving there in the late afternoon. But something on the plane caught Steve's attention, so he told me he was going to stay there and check it out, and suggested that I fly over to Victoria and visit Dad and Vera. So I did.

While I was visiting, Steve phoned me to say he had not been able to find the problem, and he didn't want me on the plane in that situation. He was going to fly airport to airport until the problem was solved. He said I should take another way to Sacramento, where he would meet me to fly the rest of the way home.

I thought that I hadn't had a nice bus ride for a long time, so I got a ticket on the Greyhound Bus to Sacramento. It was an overnight trip but I was able to get some sleep on the road. When we pulled into Sacramento, Steve was there to meet me. He had found the problem, which fortunately was minor. So I climbed back into my seat in the plane, and we headed for home base.

Thinking back, I can see how wonderfully diligent Steve was with every detail—from weight restrictions to windstorms, and awareness when things weren't quite right. He took nothing for granted, and he was always looking out for me as well. It was a wonderful and memorable trip for me with my oldest son—a very special gift never to be forgotten. I realized that Steve was not just a conscientious and highly competent pilot, he was a thoughtful and gracious human being. It reminded me of his grandfathers, both of them moved to serve with deeply compassionate care those around them, whatever the need.

When we started back to our daily routine, I found that I was getting weary of the constant work to take care of the property even with the help of Steve and Dale. A very important second reason was that Jason was now a toddler, and there were dangerous parts of this place, such as the pool whether empty or full. So it came time to decide about selling it.

One morning Steve came to me to tell me that he had decided to move on to board with a man who was a professional concert pianist. The Lord had already let me know that this would happen, so I was not unprepared to hear him and give him my blessing.

We contacted Norma to put our property on the market. I was praying, "Lord, it was so hard getting into this place, would you please make it easier to move out?" That was one prayer that God did not answer with a "Yes," for it turned out to be equally as hard, if not more so, than moving in.

I am placing a writing from the Lord here, though It came later. It shows me the heart of God, and I think it's helpful to see things from His perspective, for every one of us has been in a situation where we need the Lord to graciously remind us that He is our burden bearer.

You Need Not Carry Your Load

"My child, lift up your head. Do not lift up your heavy load for I AM with you to preserve you. I have said that I will bear your burden. If you insist on carrying it, I cannot.

"Bring your burden to Me. Bring your cares and woes to Me. I will deal with them for you and in their place I will give you tranquility and strength. Your strength is dissipated by those cares and woes. Only a glad heart will find new strength. That is why I tell you not to be anxious.

"Many burdens you carry have no basis in fact. I have promised to guide you continually and to provide every need. The trials I allow you to have do not preclude Me from fulfilling those promises. Therefore, your cares are groundless and your burdens unnecessary.

"You are here for a short time only. Your entrance into My eternal realm brings you into an eternal life and everlasting reality where there is no want, no care and no anxiety.

"Therefore, learn to abide in Me. Let My Word fill your heart and mind. Let them prepare you for that eternal life which you now have so that when you approach My Father's Throne you will come with joy and maturity of faith."

Since Dale had bought the Lock and Key business in Corona, he and his family needed to find a home there where he would be on site to manage this new venture. One day he and Elizabeth decided they were going to Corona with Norma to look for property and suggested that I go as well to look around and see if there was a place I would like to buy.

Whenever I had a big decision to make, the first thing I did was to pray about it, and I had been praying about where to move. I thought a condominium would be just fine. Somebody else would do all the yard work.

It seems the Lord was saying it was time for the family to move ahead to the new plans He had for each of us. Steve had moved into an apartment, Dale and Elizabeth were starting out as business owners, and Michael and I had moved close by in a lovely, spacious unit with a view of orange groves. We all lived close enough that we could still get together.

I was still working at Avery, enjoying my job and co-workers. There were several Christians among them, and we formed a group to have a Bible Study once a week led by one of the managers in his office. That was a time when to have such a group at a business was quite legal and nobody had a problem with it.

During this period of my life, I had the freedom and, because of the sale of the Fontana property, the money to take a vacation, so I went to Australia and New Zealand. I wish I could tell you about it here, or about the new grandchildren that were added to the family. I'll simply say those were wonderful times that greatly enriched my life.

Settled In Corona, CA

After all the moving around in the last several years, it was wonderful to be in a beautiful home where life was back on a normal rhythm and schedule. Everyone was in a new setting and doing well in their daily work.

Several months later, Elizabeth called to tell me that Hospice was starting a group in Corona and were looking for volunteers. She thought I would be good at that and suggested I check into what they did. I found that there would be ten weekly sessions of training and then we would be assigned to a patient with whom we would give information on the ending of life.

That sounded interesting as something new, and since it was in Corona, it would be convenient to take the training. I signed up, and then was assigned to a patient, or "Client." I visited them and talked with them about their needs, and what their hopes were, and did what I could do for them.

In the following year, the Hospice Director told us that a new program called Grief Share was being set up in Orange County.

The head of that program was going to have a meeting in Corona to tell us what the purpose was.

On the night of the meeting I saw several of the ladies I knew, but they were all talking together and I didn't want to break it up, so I looked around, and saw a couple sitting alone. I sat by the lady. She introduced herself and the gentleman sitting next to her. We chatted a few moments until the meeting started. At the end of the meeting, I wanted to get home, so I didn't stay for coffee or to talk to the ladies I knew.

The next spring, the Director said that every Hospice volunteer had to have a picture ID in the event they needed to visit their client in the hospital. I took the morning off work and went to the hospital to talk to the Director and get my ID. She was not there, but her secretary was. To my surprise, the secretary was the lady I had sat next to at the meeting about Grief Share.

We started talking and the conversation got around to trying to find a possible mate. She was looking on the new dating sites on the computers, but not finding much help. She suggested I try it, but that was not something I wanted to get involved with. I told her there were no prospects at work, or at church.

Then she said, "Do you remember the man I sat with at the Grief Share meeting?" I said that I didn't. She replied that he was a friend, not her husband as I had assumed. His name was Dick. She asked, "Would you mind if I give him your telephone number?" Thinking that nothing else had worked, I gave her my number.

Just a few days later, Dick phoned me and asked if I would go with him for coffee. I said I would. He picked me up at my home, and as we drove over to Riverside for coffee and ice cream, he told me his story. His wife had died two years before, he had no children and he was retired, along with a few other comments.

Then it was my turn. I told him my husband was a pastor. He didn't gulp or try to look good, and I went on to tell him that I went to the nearby prison for drug addicts to counsel with whoever wanted to talk to me. He didn't make any comment then either and I thought, "Maybe there's some hope for this guy."

As we continued to talk, I learned he lived only a mile from me in Corona. He had a brother and sister-in-law also living in Corona. I did not know anyone he knew. I told him about my family, that my father-in-law was living with me. He did not know anyone I knew either. The only person we had in common was the lady he was with at the Grief Share meeting. At the end of our visit, we agreed we had a very nice time, and he asked me if I would go with him again, and I said I would.

Dick and I went out a few more times, and then he started coming over to my house a couple of evenings a week. I began praying about Dick, because I knew almost nothing about him as a person. He was nice looking, pleasant, gentlemanly, and companionable, but that doesn't necessarily mean he would be a good husband.

While I was praying, God started giving me insights into Dick's character which I jotted down on paper. I also asked Michael what he thought about Dick, as Michael was a pretty good judge of people.

One evening Dick came over and I mentioned to him about a neighbor's bush that was growing in my back yard flower bed. I had no garden implements to cut it away. Dick said he would come the next evening and take care of it for me.

The evening was lovely as Michael and I sat in the patio watching Dick cut away the offending bush. I noticed how well he did it—no wasted movements, he knew exactly what to do. When all the cutting was done, he gathered the branches, wrapped them up and took them home to dispose of them. I thought that was great—he offered to help, and did so right away, and did it very well, leaving my flower bed looking much better.

Another time, on a weekend, I was going to make a pot of soup for Michael to eat for his lunches while I was at work. Again, Dick said he would come and help me. The sink was next to the stove on the left with a long counter on the right side. I got the soup ingredients and the pot out ready to start. The vegetables were cut up and we were moving back and forth to the stove. I noticed that we didn't get in each others way. We had fun doing it and were talking easily. Another plus for Dick.

I love to tell this story. Michael had a favorite cafeteria in Pasadena. He wanted to go there one Friday night, but I was too tired from my weekly commute to drive another long distance. Dick was there and offered to take us on Saturday.

We were sitting at the table eating our meal when Michael looked at Dick and said, "Well, are you going to marry her?" I was embarrassed and looked for a hole in the floor. Then I thought "Well, no, he's an adult. Let's see what he says." Dick looked back at Michael and calmly said, "I don't think I know her well enough yet." In my mind, I cheered at Dick's very valid response. And another plus for him.

We enjoyed each other's company, got to know each other's friends, attended each other's church, and our relationship continued to the point where we started talking about marriage. I had to consider what my sons would think and what to do about Michael if I married. I did call each of my sons to ask them if they had any reservations about my marrying Dick. Each of them said they were happy for me if that was what I wanted to do.

The Lord stepped in here as I continued praying, and gave me a Writing that was a real encouragement to my heart. This is what it said:

"My Child,

"This marriage is of me, saith the Lord. I have fashioned it out of My own Being. The love which you share is from My heart and is to be used to bless and nourish those around you.

"Even as you have rejoiced in the love and presence of each other, be sure that you rejoice in the love and presence of Me, for I am the focus of your faith. I am the One who has redeemed you and fashioned you to be a unit, fit for My purposes.

"Be sure that you make room for Me in your love. Do not take that which I have given and use it only for yourselves. Offer it back in praise to Me and I will multiply it and keep it fresh and new for you. My love through you is to be warmth and light to others who will find their way to Me by it.

"Remain in an attitude of gratitude and thanksgiving and I will bless you and your home with peace, joy, and love."

My dad came down to be a part of our ceremony at my church with my pastor. My best friend Jackie Klein was my Matron of Honor, John's daughters Shannon and Robin were the flower girls, and Dale's son Jason was the ring bearer. Dick's brother Dan was his best man and his brother-in-law Tab and Steve were the ushers. At the end, I was introduced as Mrs. Darda Burkhart.

I was glad that my new friends could meet my dad.

Michael tried living in a senior housing complex but he didn't like it, so Elizabeth did what she had promised to do if he ever needed a place to stay; she took him to live with her. That worked well for him. He preferred being with family, and by then they had known one another for many years.

Dick and I decided that I would move into his home, which was only a few blocks away. Since his house was fully furnished, I gave my furniture to John and Caprice. About all that I moved over were my personal belongings and my pictures to decorate the walls. Dick said I could put my pictures wherever I wanted and change anything in the décor but I liked the way things were and so I did not change anything.

Having been previously married for a number of years, we were able to come together with few, if any, problems. We easily settled into married life and our new routines with a lot of joy and happiness. Our neighbors were very nice people, and I became friends with them.

In about July of 1990, I got a phone call that Dad had surgery and was in the hospital in Victoria. I flew there to visit him and see how he was recuperating. I'm not sure what the surgery was for, but he came through it pretty well. The wife of another patient in his room took me out to the hall to warn me about the effects the anaesthetic had on her husband. I thanked her for that information, but thought that Dad was too clear-minded to be affected. However, he did show some of the same symptoms as her husband. I was there when the doctor came in to check on his progress. It was interesting to watch Dad sit up straight on the side of the bed and answer the questions correctly.

When I went home I kept in touch with Dad by phone. He seemed to be recuperating well, and able to keep a close watch on Vera for her forgetfulness. She was having trouble with Dementia. It all seemed to be going well until October. I was told that Dad had said he was tired and laid down on the couch for a rest. He slept, and woke up in Heaven and in the presence of the Lord he loved so dearly and served so mightily.

I flew back to Victoria for the funeral and to stay with Vera during the daytime. The Funeral Chapel was packed with people who loved Percy and respected him highly for his service to the Lord and most everyone he met. Two local pastors were in charge of the service. Several people gave their eulogies, including two of his grandchildren. It was a memorable time of both grieving and rejoicing that Percy was now at home with the Lord he loved so completely. What a reunion he must have had with his wife Margarette and the hundreds of others he'd served and loved into the Kingdom. He was buried next to my mother in the local cemetery.

When Dad died, I lost my spiritual counselor. Dad was a rare man. He seemed to see a need, and pray about it seeking God's purpose. Then he had the gift of faith to tackle the project and see it through any obstacles to completion. At his funeral one of my nephews commented that Bumpa always seemed to know when he needed help. The same awareness of need was evident on the mission field. Dad won the respect of so many on the coast, or wherever he went, because he exemplified Jesus every day.

Looking back to that time, I wish he had told us more about what he really did and the many dangers he faced day and night on the Messenger III and how God protected him and the crew every time they left a city or village port. I would then have felt closer to him because of what he went through in his spiritual life, moving on from there to feeling closer to my Heavenly Father and how much He went through to give me salvation.

Back home, I was thinking of Dad and his ministry, and I had the sense that God had passed his prayer mantle to me. Prayer was always a resort to me whenever I needed something, even in my younger years. Today, I still have people asking me to pray with them. At church, the Bible studies I would like to attend were always at the same time as the prayer meetings, and I always chose to pray. That was my choice. I now realize it is also my calling.

That year John and Caprice decided to move up to Washington State, close to the Canadian Border. For several years during their time living in Santa Barbara County, their little family had gone to visit their cousins in Victoria, B.C., just as Bob and I had done with our children when they were young. John was hired by a sheriff's department in Washington and left the sunny coast of California.

Moving from Southern California to Washington State is a big change in more ways than geographic. The family had previously only seen the new area in the summertime when it's lovely weather with long days and lots of sunshine. In the winter, the days are short, there is lots of rain and cold, windy, snowy weather. Sometimes the snow is too deep to get out of the house for several days.

One day Bill, a fellow Deputy Sheriff, told John there was an opening in Lynden for a Lieutenant Police Officer, and suggested that he apply for it. (This kind man turned out to be my neighbor when I moved to Lynden in 2005.)

John was hired by the Lynden Police Department as a Lieutenant. The city was small, only about 5,000 population. I think he was employee #8. At that time the Police Department was in a small building with a jail cell in the lower floor.

John brought a great deal of experience to the department in areas that were not necessary in this small town at the time, but would be later on as the town grew in size, such as marijuana cultivation, SWAT team training, and background investigations on potential new hires.

I retired from Avery the next year, but what I thought would be smooth sailing was marked by Jason's horrific accident. It was so close to being fatal. His story is in this book, but I want to add additional details here.

For two months Dick and I spent each day at the hospital with the other family members, taking turns to visit Jason in the ICU, praying desperately to God for his healing, continuing into his time at the hospital when he went for rehabilitation therapies. Dick was a real support for me at this terrible time. Elizabeth's family was with her, so Dick and I concentrated on Dale. It was such an emotional drain on all of us.

Because of his injuries, Jason could not have navigated the crowded halls and extensive grounds at Corona High, so Elizabeth's parents, Norma and Bill, invited him to live with them in Lucerne in Northern California. It was a big change for him. Lake County is an agricultural community with a small population. There are mountains, a large ancient lake, a lot of wild animals, open spaces, and country folk. The pace was slower. The entire student body at Upper Lake High School, where he would go, was only 305 students, and Jason graduated in a class of only 60 to 70 kids.

This move turned out to be extremely significant for our family—particularly Dale's and Jason's, but it affected me deeply as well. Looking back, I see God's hand in taking Jason into a different world. One thing that had troubled me was the influences he was exposed to. At the time he was in middle school, Satanic music was becoming very popular, and Jason was caught up in it.

I wondered what I could do about it. One day a thought came about doing a "Jericho" walk around the school. But how could I do it quietly without drawing attention to what I was doing? I wouldn't know how to explain it to anyone. Dick played golf twice a week and was gone for several hours, so I decided to do the walks on those days. I would walk around the school block seven days praying against the effects of that music on the students, and I also prayed in the Spirit because I didn't know what else to pray about. I don't know what effects my prayers had, except that Jason was now out of that demonic influence.

Teen years are a time of vulnerability when children are beginning to grow up. The influences of that time can be incorporated into their being the rest of their lives. I look at Jason today, at the outstanding man of God he has become, and wonder what he might have been if he had not moved to the other end of the state. It isn't that God caused that horrific accident, but He certainly used it to bring astonishing good into many lives because of it.

When Jason moved to Northern California to live with his grandparents, Dale followed him so he could continue to care for his son who still needed therapies. He left the business to Elizabeth, packed up his belongings and tools, and drove his truck there.

It was a difficult start-over time for Dale. To pay for Jason's needs, he took any job he could, whatever it might be. It was a while until he found a locksmith with whom he could work. Once he started that work, he was back in his own territory, and it was not long before he was able to strike out and form his own business, known as Lake County Lock and Safe. Word got around about the excellence of his work and the wide range of his knowledge of locksmithing. Dale's work was mobile. He had a big truck with his company name printed on it. He drove to customers from place to place, learning the geography of the county as he went. He became respected for his reliability and integrity, and also his calm presence and gentle humor—something that was sorely needed in situations where hostility or emergency were aspects of the job. His business began to thrive and he was able to fully care for all of Jason's needs.

Dale loved the area and knew he wanted to settle there for good. Since he and Elizabeth were separated and the marriage had fallen apart, he filed for divorce and it was granted.

After a while, Dale was introduced to a lady name Jillian. She was Executive Director of the Lake County Arts Council in Lakeport and well known for her interest in the arts and artists in the area. They became friends and that friendship blossomed into a loving relationship that ended up in a marriage that was made in Heaven. Through Jillian, Dale was plunged into the artistic community, which had musicians, writers, artists, poets, actors, and others. Jillian's superb organizational skills and magnetic personality drew gifted individuals out of isolation and into the community of creative people that inspired one another. And Dale met them all. He loved it.

One of them was a writer and musician named Carolyn Wing Greenlee, who had become one of Jillian's close friends. When Carolyn told her that their band was looking for a bass player, Jillian immediately told her about Dale, whose musical abilities and easygoing personality quickly earned him a place in the band Tied To The Stone. With them he recorded "Time of Light," an album of original songs by Carolyn's friend, singer/songwriter Dan Worley. That was the start of a friendship that would change their lives, and the lives of our family, in profound and surprising ways.

Dale's bass playing is inspired—he doesn't read music notes, he hears it in his head. He's always humming bass parts, and is considered one of the best base guitarists in the area. He has been asked to sit in with several other bands and plays regularly with the popular Lake County Diamonds.

Jillian was careful in getting to know Jason who was not sure about this new wife for his dad. She told him she was not his mother, but she would be a friend to him if he wanted her to be. She was loving toward him, and he began to love her back for the way she treated him as an adult. They became a close family as a result.

I met Jillian when I visited Dale for a few days on his birthday. She was a very pleasant person—quick to welcome people and enjoy their company. She and Dale complemented one another in their personalities. I knew they would have a good life together.

In 1991, Steve's project in Holland was completed, and he came back to the plant in Painesville, Ohio, where he worked prior to the job in Holland. He bought his first home in a little town called Chardon. He reconnected with his glider friends and was soon back flying when the weather permitted.

When Steve bought his first home, the mother in me wanted to see what her son had gotten himself into. Dick was from Ohio and moved to California after high school. So we thought we would take a vacation and asked if we could spend a few days with Steve, and also visit Dick's friends in his home town, Marysville.

Steve's new home was a very nice house with a cozy feel to it. Dick and I prayed over this new home asking God to bless it and that His presence would protect Steve and his new property. Then Dick and I drove to Marysville where Dick reconnected with dear friends after so many years. Then we flew home.

When our plane landed, Dick's brother Dan and his wife Esther met us at the airport with some bad news. Our house had been broken into while we were gone. We were shocked because Dick had been very careful to be sure the house was locked and protected before we left.

We had to list everything that was taken, mostly my jewelry and my early type of computer on which I had typed a lot of my writings. The value of what was taken amounted to $5,000. I grieved over the loss of family jewelry that was special to me and could not be replaced. A few mornings later, sitting at breakfast, I heard God speak audibly to me with my father's voice, "Oh, honey, let it go. Let it go." That is just what he would have said if he were alive, and strangely, it comforted me and I could let the sorrow go for peace to come in.

As a new retiree, I would often sit in our den and say to Dick, "I feel like I should be doing something." He would reply, "Why? You're retired." Then I relaxed and enjoyed the two of us sitting in our chairs looking out at the humming birds feeding just outside the glass doors.

Since Dick played golf two mornings a week, I joined a Women's Bible Study at our church. I hadn't been able to do that for years, and it was so good to be in a group of women who also loved the Lord, and learn the richness of God's Word by a capable teacher. I made new friends and I am still in touch with some of them at this time.

At the same time, Michael was still living with Elizabeth, who was now caring for him as he began to fail in his health. He often asked, "Why is God mad at me that He doesn't take me home?" His longing to be "at home" with Jesus was finally granted, and he passed away. We had a funeral service for him and he was buried in the family plot at Forest Lawn Cemetery. He left quite a legacy of missionary work among the Slavic people.

I heard that my brother Frank was having silent heart attacks. He worked through them not knowing what was happening. Then he became unable to work, and had a lot of pain. He finally went to a Cardiologist who informed him that his heart was badly weakened by the attacks. His wife Sheila took care of him even though she had a full-time job. He finally succumbed and passed away. It was a great loss to our whole family and we grieved deeply for him.

Once more, I flew to Victoria to be there for the funeral and be with my family at this very sad time. For us who cling to Christ, there is always the comfort of knowing that death is not the end. We knew Frank was with Jesus, rejoicing with Dad and Mother once more.

John and Caprice's children were growing up. Shannon was a student at University of Washington. Robin was finishing high school and Brandon was just entering high school. When Shannon became engaged to Jered, another student at the university, John had a long, stern talk with the young man to make sure he was the right one to marry his beloved daughter. The Bible says it is a blessing to see your children's children. I had that blessing, and the joy of knowing they were also followers of Jesus Christ.

THE NEW CENTURY

There was a lot of discussion in the news as to how technology would be able to handle the change of years from 1999 to 2000. There were concerns whether the computers and other technology machines would be able to have a smooth transition or if there would be problems with the way the machines were programmed. Fortunately, the changeover went very smoothly, and all those involved in that technology breathed a great sigh of relief.

But not everything was able to continue to function well. Dick began having some physical problems that caused us to go to the doctor. The testing determined that he had prostate cancer. We sought the advice of a Urologist who laid out the plans available for his treatment. He told Dick that it was a slow-growing tumor, and he could choose between chemo or radiation to deal with the cancer.

Dick chose to have radiation, and after a course of several days of radiation, he felt better. The doctor said that the cancer was taken care of, and Dick should be fine. We were relieved with this report, and Dick returned to his golfing schedule and I to my Women's Bible Study at the church and prayer meeting in a home.

Sometime during the next year or so, I had a slight inkling of a possible move for us. It was nothing more than the seed of an idea, but I pondered it from time to time. There was no real reason to move, but the traffic was getting so heavy that you needed to pick your hours to be on the freeway so you could do your errands before rush hour began with stop-and-go travel.

Steve was offered a job in Seattle and decided to accept it. It seemed the family was moving north. Meanwhile the thought of moving kept coming back to my mind, and I started to talk with Dick about the possibility. He was the original owner of his home, and had lived in Corona for at least 50 years, so it would be a big adjustment for him. If we did move, where would we go? The U.S. is a big place and we had no idea of living anywhere else, so we started praying about it.

As we progressed into 2004, the thought of moving became stronger. As we prayed, the Lord started giving me encouraging personal writings from time to time. I wrote them down and read them often for the comfort they gave us. In one of them were the words, "Your children will welcome you." What a great thing to read for the directions it gave us.

After talking with Steve and Dale, we realized we were not meant to move near them. That meant John would be the one to contact about our move.

One Sunday morning at church, the Scripture reading was the Christmas story from Luke, chapter one. When I read in my Bible verse 45, it leaped off the page to me. "Blessed is she who has believed that what the Lord has said to her will be accomplished." What a confirmation that we were on the right track, so to speak! That lifted a big load from us, and more peace was in our hearts.

Another confirmation came a little later, again from the Scriptures. In Mark 16:7, an angel in the tomb told the women who had come to anoint Jesus' body, "But go, tell His disciples and Peter that He is going before you to Galilee. There you will see Him, just as He told you." When I read that, I thought, "Wow. Galilee was their home area." My home area was Victoria/Vancouver, close to the Pacific Northwest.

Dick and I went to look for a place to live in Lynden. A real estate agent showed us around, and we really liked one house in particular. The house was in a 55+ Active Senior complex, in a neighborhood of larger homes. I knew this was the house the Lord had kept for us. It was move-in ready. The paint was fresh, the carpet was good. That was a really important thing in our consideration of this house.

The next morning we flew back to Corona to decide about the purchase of the new house. I asked Dick what he thought about buying it. After all, if we moved there I was "going home," but he would be leaving his family, golf buddies, and friends—everything and everyone he had known for the last fifty years. In a loving voice he said, "This house means nothing to me." Even though he was experiencing Dementia, he clearly meant what he said.

A few days later, I had a phone call from the Real Estate Agent to say that if we wanted to buy the house, we should act on it because the price had just dropped $13,000. Over the phone, I told her we would buy it. Another sign from the Lord that this was the place we would move to. He also gave me a Writing about the move. With those words of encouragement, I called a couple of moving companies to get an estimate from them. I expected it would be several thousand dollars.

Then Dale called and said his friend Rick in Upper Lake, California, had a moving company and I should call him and see what he could do. I thought that Rick was too far away to take the job. Besides that, we needed someone who would also pack us up, for that was too big a job for us.

When I talked to Rick, he said he and his partner would pack us up and move us. I asked about insuring our belongings and he said that he carried the insurance, so I did not have to be concerned about it. He also offered to trail our car. Finally, I agreed to his offer to move us.

It was hard to say good-bye to Dick's brother and sister-in-law, knowing the separation would be for a long time. We invited them to come and visit us in Lynden, and they promised they would.

Rick packed our things and started the long drive north, and Dick and I flew to Washington where we stayed with John and Caprice till our furniture arrived. We were surprised when we got a phone call that Rick was almost there. John, Caprice, Dick and I rushed over to open up the house. Only a few minutes later Rick drove up, ready to unload. It wasn't long before all the labeled boxes were in the right rooms and the furniture was in place, the beds were ready to be set up, and the car was in the garage.

Rick presented his bill, and I looked it over. I was surprised that the total was less than the estimates I had received from the other moving companies, even though he had trailed our car, something that was not included in the other estimates. I wrote out a check for him and thanked him profusely for all he had done for us. Dale's friend had been faster, more efficient, and less expensive than what we could imagine, and it was a huge blessing from the Lord Who was, once again, overseeing another God-ordained move in life.

One day not long after moving in, Dick and I were walking around the complex and saw a neighbor working in his flower garden. We started talking to him. He was very friendly. He said that he used to live in Port Alberni, B.C., located on Vancouver Island. I asked him if he knew of Percy Wills. "Oh yes, I knew Percy," he said. I told him Percy was my father, and that opened quite a conversation about our families.

We decided to try one of the churches that was much like the one we left in Corona. The service was good and the people welcomed us warmly. The Pastor gave a good message, and so we continued to worship there.

Dick adjusted pretty well to the new location. We drove around the area to see the natural beauty in this section of the Pacific Northwest. Lots of trees, mountains to the north and east, and the ocean only a few miles to the west. It was truly a most pleasant location.

Dick's brother Dan had promised to come and see us when we were settled. He came in February for a few days. We showed him around the town and countryside that was so spacious and different from Corona. He was pleased to see that Dick was doing so well.

Throughout the years, more babies had been added to the family and the first ones had grown up so fast. My granddaughter Robin was engaged to Alan Coombs, whom she had met the previous summer at a Children's Summer Camp in Bellingham. She was the nurse on duty, and he was hired to be the lifeguard at the lake. Of course John took Alan to lunch and had a long and serious talk with him about being a good husband to his precious daughter. They were married at the camp grounds where they had met. During these years, I attended weddings, visited new (and older) grandchildren, and marveled at the wonderful spouses my offspring had chosen. One couple had told the Lord they would trust Him for their mate and not seek one on their own. God brought Brandon and Esther together and gave them three beautiful children. Are there any riches greater than these—that your family members would choose to spend their lives living in the light of the One Who created them?

That summer, Dick was not feeling well. We went to the doctor who told me that his cancer had returned. That was a surprise because his tests had always come back in the normal range.

One morning in November Dick wasn't hungry for breakfast. Suddenly, he had a severe attack and was bleeding. I immediately called 911, then I called John who came over to be with me at the hospital.

I knew I could not take care of Dick at home so we arranged for him to be moved from there to a local facility where he would have the care he needed. I don't think he was aware of what was going on when he arrived there. I spent time with him, then went home for the night. The next morning I went over to be with him but he was still silent. At noon I went home for a short period of time when the phone rang. It was the nurse telling me that Dick had just passed away. It was the 2nd of November, 2006. I called John to let him know, and he and Caprice met me there, as I grieved for him.

The next week we had a family memorial for Dick, just John, Caprice, Robin, and me. I also arranged for a memorial service in Corona where Dick had lived so many years. His brother Dan was there and so many friends, and I wanted them to be able to honor him there.

The day of the memorial was a lovely warm, sunny California kind of day. The scenery before us was majestic and we all had a sense of peace and beauty. I don't know how they found out, but several people who had been members of the church Bob had pastored in Monterey Park attended the service. It was so good to see them and recall our memories of those special times when God's presence and His love was so strong in the meetings. Several said they had not found another church like ours.

I was surrounded by loving people, but when the time of gathering was over, I said my farewells to Dan and his family and to my long-time friends from many years back and flew home the next day. Once again, I was alone.

A New Single Life And Challenge

John was at the airport to greet me and take me home. The house was lonesome without Dick sitting there. I knew I was going to have to get used to single life once more. What do I do with my time now that I didn't have Dick to care for? I was still grieving and was not sure what I wanted to do.

I volunteered at our church as a Greeter to welcome people entering the sanctuary prior to the service. I joined a weekly prayer group at the church and got to know some of the people.

After a while an announcement was made that Jeanne, one of the church members who was a published author, was forming a class in Creative Writing. A friend of mine told me she was going to sign up and suggested that I do so as well. That sounded interesting and would give me something to do that was worthwhile.

Jeanne explained the purpose for the class, and gave us an outline of what we would be learning. At the end of the class she asked me, "Have you ever thought about writing a book?" The question startled me. I said that I hadn't, and then we ended the conversation.

But the question would not leave me. What on earth would I write about—my life was mundane. I had nothing unusual to write even a few pages, let alone a whole book. As was my practice, I started praying for insight and wisdom, what to do about this question.

The Lord brought to my mind my father's missionary activity on the west coast of Vancouver Island. The area was isolated, frequented by severe storms at sea, had no roads, but most of all, no message of the Gospel had been given to them. That is what God called Dad to do. It was a life worthy of being put into print. My question was, how do I do it? I had no knowledge of writing that big of a project. I continued in prayer and God started putting the pieces together for me.

I bought a notebook and started writing—where? At the beginning, of course. I wrote about Dad's family and his early days in Victoria, and how he met my mother, Margarette. I hadn't gotten far into that part when I realized I would need to buy a computer system and learn how to use it. Then I went to the local thrift store to buy a desk to put it on.

Once that was all installed, I turned to my friend and neighbor, Joan, who was experienced on a computer. She was such a big help in getting me familiar with using a computer, how to set up a page to write on, how to be sure to save what I had written, etc., etc. Once I had all that in mind, I got my written notes and typed them into the computer, and started to document my story. I felt like a child going to kindergarten for the first time learning my numbers and colors.

Although I was very familiar with Dad's and Mother's histories, when I had to start writing about the intervening years of their marriage, I had no information of that time period and didn't know where I could get it. My parents and my brother Frank were in Heaven. My aunt Mildred had some information, but she would have been too young to know the details I needed. I turned this over to the Lord in prayer, because without it there could be no book.

In April of 2008, the Esperanza ministry stepped away from the Shantymen's Christian Association, and became a separate mission on its own, known as Esperanza Ministries. They were having their first annual business meeting as the new organization and their donors were invited to attend the meeting at the mission base in Esperanza. John decided he would like to go and asked if I wanted to join him. I had never been there, and now I had time to go.

I thought it would be nice to leave a few days early to visit my friends at the Coastal Missions base in Chemainus on Vancouver Island, and then meet John at the Ferry Dock in nearby Nanaimo for our trip. It was so good to see these dear friends of many years who were well acquainted with the Esperanza Mission. We had a great time as I added another pair of hands to their daily work. We talked about what they were doing and where they were heading when the boat work started again.

The day I was leaving, the President of the Mission, "Uncle" Roy, as everyone called him, said he had something for me. He handed me some file folders, saying that Dad had left them with him several years earlier and told him, "You will know who to give them to." That's all he said to "Uncle" Roy. One of the folders had the year 1979 written on it, but he did not tell me when Dad gave them to him. I took the folders with awe and deep thanks, then put them in my suitcase and said goodbye to all of them in time to pick up John for the rest of our journey.

We drove north to the city of Campbell River, then turned west on the highway leading to the other side of the Island. Parts of the scenery were stunning—large lakes ringed by high mountains with only an occasional settlement to pass through on a winding road that led to the town of Tahsis. That was the end of the highway and we had to park the car and carry our luggage down to the wharf where the boats from Esperanza were awaiting us.

The people attending the meeting came from many places in Canada and the U.S. Although we did not know each other, we were united in our love and concern for the well-being and ongoing work among the people there. The mission that began in 1930 had grown in size and spiritual importance over the years and we all wanted it to continue to grow in reaching many more of the people for our Savior, Jesus Christ.

The business meeting went well and great support was given to this new start of the older mission. Now it could stand on its own under God's direction.

The trip was so full of activity that I did not have time to really look at and read what the folders contained. When I got home, I finally had a chance to look over the papers I had in my suitcase. There were many sheets of Dad's writings about things he saw and was involved in on the coast. There were proofed carbon copies of the text of the book *Splendour From The Sea*, written by W. Phillip Keller and published in 1963, and now out of print. Apparently, Dad had given the author a lot of the stories in the book. I continued to go through my dad's papers fascinated by everything I read.

Then I opened another folder, and here were Dad's stories about his early life, following his discharge from the Army at the end of WWI. I couldn't put the papers down! I was thrilled to pieces at the sheer gold I held in my hands. God must have been chuckling in Heaven when He gave me the answer to my prayers.

There were so many stories that I could choose the ones that fit my need. Stories about working in the harvests for farmers in the Prairie provinces, sorting potatoes, even being scammed by a traveling salesman selling winter coats that never arrived. Stories about meeting Mother and their wedding. All that I read was so pertinent to my needs of that era, that I could just copy what he had already written—and much better than I could have worded them. I finally put them carefully in a safe place and got ready for my annual visit to see Dale and Jillian for his birthday.

While I was visiting Dale, he introduced me to their friend, Carolyn Wing Greenlee. Dale had told her some of the stories of his grandfather's life and she was intrigued to meet someone who had actually lived through many miracles. She was an author of many books and had for decades taught writing and helped people get their stories organized into books.

Carolyn recommended that I attend the annual Women Writing the West Conference. That year it was being held in San Antonio, Texas. She said there would be panels of literary agents, editors, and publishers, each one looking for good books. Attendees could make a 10-minute appointment with whomever they chose, and it was all included in the conference fee.

I took the opportunity to make an appointment with an editor to gain some help for my writing. Her first question was "What's your hook?" I asked her what she meant by that. She replied that the very first sentence has to be one that catches the readers imagination and draws them into further reading. I thought of what I already had written and said to myself, *Oh no! Now I have to rewrite my two chapters.* She kindly went on and gave me some more tips and suggestions for me to use when I went home.

The members of WWW ranged from the "pre-published" neophytes like me to multiple-award-winning Jane Kirkpatrick, who has more than 30 books in print. All of them were quick to welcome me and nobody acted like a big shot. They were like a big family.

Some of the presenters taught sessions on ways to market your book because, I found out to my dismay, the publishers pretty much left that task to the author. I always thought the advantage to having a "real" publisher was distribution, but all of the presenters quickly dispelled that belief. Writers were tending to find their placement with small, independent publishers and even "vanity press," the name given to companies the author pays to publish the book.

Carolyn's friend, David Balsiger, was one of the presenters at the conference. He was a Times Best Selling author many times over, and he was very knowledgeable about the book business. The three of us spent a lot of time together, both at the conference and visiting the Alamo and the River Walk. David answered all my questions, clarifying options and alerting me to hazards and pitfalls.

Carolyn and I became good friends on this trip. We roomed together, and neither of us got much sleep because we would lie on our beds in the dark talking about writing my book. She was very interested to hear my stories and helped me see how to present them in the most effective ways.

The next year the WWW conference was held at UCLA in Los Angeles, California. It was 2009 and I roomed with Carolyn and her brand-new guide dog Hedy. By law, service dogs are allowed to go wherever their partner goes. It was fun to have a dog with us, but Carolyn was worried. Where would she be able to relieve Hedy? In some areas, the campus of UCLA is like a huge city of tall buildings with concrete between—not one blade of grass or beds of shrubs and bushes. I remember walking from the registration desk out into the walkways our first day there. Immediately in front of us was a long rectangular planter filled with live bamboo. It was perfect. Carolyn had plastic bags, Hedy did her business on cue, and the need was met. I don't remember seeing any other planters like that the whole time we were there, but we needed just one.

It may seem a trivial thing, but it wasn't to Carolyn and Hedy. It turned out to be significant for another reason. As Carolyn expressed her amazement at finding the perfect place right outside the door, I mentioned casually that this is the way the Christian life is meant to be. I said it is the normal supernatural Christian life. It was a new concept to her, but not to me. I'd grown up witnessing God's provision all my life.

As usual, the conference was full of good information, encouragement, and warm fellowship. And, as last time, we stayed up most of the night talking about my book. One thing was clear from the sessions, the big publishers were very choosy about what they risked their money on. Very few did memoirs. David Balsiger had told us even the big publishers would drop a book if it didn't get enough attention from stores and libraries, and that was before the book was even printed. The agents, editors, and publishers had very specific things they were looking for, and they wanted to know if the writer had a platform that would provide sufficient interest to generate sales that would make it worthwhile to publish that book.

Because it was so hard to get published now, alternatives were popping up. There were small, independent publishers, as I said before. Carolyn's company, Earthen Vessel Productions, was one, but it was thousands of dollars for them to publish a book, so they weren't taking on new projects. Another option was print on demand, which used to be called "vanity press." The implication was that a writer wasn't good enough to get published by a real publisher, so he or she would pay a company to do the work. Writers could choose from a list of optional services. I realized the best thing to do was print on demand.

At that time, this publishing style was new and very expensive. I finally found one. They offered two or three options I could buy for their services from start to finish of one's book. I chose the one with the most editing since it had been a really long time since I sat in a Grammar class in school.

With help from God, I found a good sentence to write as a "Hook" to start the book. I continued my writing and found that the papers that "Uncle" Roy had given me were truly invaluable.

My writing got to the point that I needed a good eye-catching title. So I started praying about it. The working title was, "Percy Wills, Pioneer Missionary" but that would not be interesting enough for someone to pick up a book and peruse it. One morning, as I woke up, clearly in my mind was the new title, "Forging Ahead for God." Perfect. I quickly thanked God for supplying that piece of key information.

The next major need was the cover. The publishing company would provide a cover if I wanted them to do it. My grandson, Brandon, is an artist, so I asked him if he wanted to design a cover. He agreed to do it, and produced a sketch of the Mission boat, Messenger III in a stormy sea with forests and clouds as a backdrop. In the lower right hand portion he drew Dad's face. When I looked at that drawing, Dad's features looked so perfect that I almost expected to hear him speak. I was so amazed at what Brandon had accomplished for the cover, I couldn't thank him enough. I submitted his sketch to the publisher and they accepted it.

The book was published in 2009. The publisher gave me a large number of free books, which were given out to family members, people who were named in the book, and some special friends. Of course it was also available for those interested in Esperanza, since *Splendor from the Sea* is out of print.

During these new decades, there were weddings and babies and the blessings of these good unions between godly young people and the children they brought into the world and nurtured in the truth of God's love for them. I will not be accounting all of them, because this book is not about that, though godly families and harmonious gatherings are becoming more rare these days. However, I do want to write about one birth, because it was another occasion for huge amounts of prayers.

Jason and his wife Melissa had been careful to get the prescribed checkups all through the pregnancy, and even on the day of delivery, the doctor said all was well with the baby. That's why it was such a shock when Joshua was born with a pulmonary-vein defect in his heart. He needed immediate surgery.

Jason phoned us with the news that he and Joshua would be airlifted to Seattle Children's Hospital for that surgery. Melissa had to have a Caesarian section so she could not come with them.

We immediately called all our family to have them pray for little Joshua and his parents. John's daughter Shannon lived in the Seattle area, so she headed for the hospital, and John also left for the same destination. Both arrived about the same time as Jason— it was near midnight. It was a blessing that Jason was sent to Seattle where our family could be such a support for him. He was very tired and very worried as to Joshua's future.

Open heart surgery began almost at once. We were so thankful that Jason did not have to go through this terrifying experience alone. Much prayer was backing him, Melissa, and Joshua during those long night hours. Finally, the surgeon came out to tell them that the surgery was successful, and that Joshua should do well. The newborn was placed in the Neonatal ICU department, hooked up to multiple wires and machines and bags of infusions, where a nurse was assigned to him. She said that vital signs were taken hourly, and her vigil was for him alone.

I drove down a day or two later and was able to visit him and see for myself how he was. As I looked at him, I could see that the incision in his chest had not been closed. It was covered, but you could see his heart beating, and view all the monitors detailing his progress.

As sore and in pain as Melissa was, she was determined to fly and join us all in Seattle. After about two weeks, Joshua was discharged. It was Christmas Eve so Jason and family stayed in Seattle and joined us for the holiday. There was constant praise and thanks to the Lord for saving Joshua's life. We wondered what God had in store for him as he grew up.

I find it interesting that Dale could have been killed even before he could walk, Jason nearly died in the horrific accident when he was a teenager, and Joshua, the third generation in this line of the family, could have died shortly after he was born. It's also interesting to note that all three of these male members of the family encounter God in supernatural ways so often. When Dale needs encouragement, he always finds two dimes—a pair of dimes—reminding him to shift to a new reality. Jillian told him they were from his grandfathers, whom he loved and respected so much, and the whimsical pun reminds Dale the same God Who gave those men the strength they needed for whatever they faced is there for him as well. For decades Jason has been getting prophetic dreams and visions, and he is a man of fervent and discerning prayer who prays with Melissa and their son Joshua especially when there is need for intercession. Joshua himself began having visions when he was six years old. He also gets words of knowledge. He is beautifully grounded in his confidence in the trustworthy character of our Savior God and he just turned twelve.

I want to mention here that I see spiritual strength throughout the individual members of our entire family line as they face hard things and dilemmas, meeting them with earnest prayers and reliance on the goodness of God. Some have gone through terrible things in extremely difficult circumstances and I am in awe at the depth of their walks with God through each life-changing decision or long-term struggle. I'm so proud of them all, and I'm sure my parents, Percy and Margarette Wills, would have been surprised and delighted to see the offspring that have come from their godly union and the legacy of prayer trusting Jesus always to hear them and respond with wisdom and love.

As I'm having to leave out the births and marriages, entrusting them to the uncut family version of my story, I am also leaving out some of the physical issues I've had since I've gotten older. Each one involved loving help from my family and wonderful doctors, and included a dislocated hip, breast cancer, and the details of the most recent one, a fractured pelvis. There was also the heartbreaking loss of Dale's beloved Jillian, whose absence we still feel deeply.

I know that everyone dies. Even Jesus died. And some die much sooner than is usual, which is a troubling truth of life. Many babies die. A teenaged girl who had the same head injury as Jason at the same time of his accident did not survive. I survived my cancer, but Jillian did not. Why? Our whole family prayed earnestly that she would recover. I flew up to help take care of her and to support Dale at the end, praying for her to rally as people sometimes do. Friends in Lake County were praying too, and one saw Jillian in a dazzling bright white robe about the time she stepped into Eternity. But we are still left with broken hearts.

There is no way to guess why some live and some die. There are no neat answers, no hints in Scripture, no promises that we will understand. Those who think they can explain what God does are missing part of the equation. God is not small enough to fit into our human understanding. And it's not particularly helpful to guess. Someone said God's plans only make sense if you know what God knows.

COVID And Other Changes

Our family kept expanding. My grandchildren had married and set up their own households. Now I had great grandchildren. When we got together, it was quite a crowd!

In August of 2019, John took the opportunity to retire from his position of Police Chief at the Lynden Police Department after forty-two years of being in law enforcement. It was God's perfect timing, for shortly after that the campaign against police authority was launched.

Then COVID-19 broke out when great fear was in all the news, and terrible things were happening all over our country and the world. We all know what that time was like and how deeply it affected every member of the family in one way or another. Many people are still trying to get over the results of that fearsome disease and reconcile with one another.

I have heard that terrible conflicts over the vaccine divided families, friends, even churches, but we were not disrupted like that. We trusted God with our lives, and the matter was taken to God in prayer. Some of our family were vaccinated and the rest were not. Some of the ones who were vaccinated rested on the Scripture in Mark 16: 17, where Jesus talks to His disciples after his resurrection. "In My name they will cast out demons, In new languages they will speak. Snakes they will pick up, and if they drink anything deadly, it will positively not harm them." (Wuest) No one who worked lost their job. We remained healthy and gave great thanks to God for His mercy.

Stuck at home amidst confusion, quarantines, lockdowns, and conflicting reports and controversy about masks and gatherings, my friend Carolyn decided to write another book, one with stories of God's miraculous workings in the lives of ordinary human beings. She called it *MIGHTY: Vision for the Supernatural Normal Christian Life*. She said she had been thinking about that concept ever since we roomed together at WWW, and had subsequently seen evidence of that miraculous Presence in her own life. She also wanted to include the stories of other eyewitnesses, and asked if I would write up the account of my father's founding of Esperanza by faith, and the remarkable last dinner at Emmaeus, the house on Belmont, where the two servicemen stood up and said they were the ones who had written the Scriptures and their names in the pagoda in Hong Kong. I had written these stories for my other book, but she asked for details that made me have to search my memory—things such as what we fed them and how we decorated the house for Christmas. As she sent questions in emails, I began to get details from the archives of my memories of the early days during that very special ministry of which I, a teenaged girl, was a part. I hadn't worked on any writing since the book on my dad's ministry, but I found I hadn't forgotten, and Carolyn's questions made each of those stories more vibrant.

Then, in early 2021, I was working in the kitchen when I tripped and fell to the floor. I dragged myself to where I could get the phone to call 911 and John. At the ER, a CT Scan showed that

I had broken a bone in my right pelvic area. I was sent to Seattle for surgery.

As always, much prayer went up on my behalf and I came through well, though months of healing and rehab lay ahead. Everyone was nice, well-trained, and I received excellent care, but I was bored. I was used to a lot of activity, family, my church and the two prayer groups I attended each week. Whether I wanted it or not, I found myself mostly alone with God.

The significance of this forced hiatus in my busy life was it opened new things. I was serious about following Jesus, and had spent my life serving wherever He led, and I had an excellent foundation in faith, but still hungered for more—deeper communion with God, greater understanding of Scriptures, more powerful ways to pray. When I was still quite young, I had become a pastor's wife, and there were holes in my understanding I didn't have time to fill. This period of confinement in the rehab facility was God's gift to me. It was my time to be alone with Him.

It seemed like an awfully long time that I was in rehab, and I was anxious to get back to "real life," but now I see how God used that time of confinement to give me something I had been wanting since I was a young woman just graduating from Bible college. He doesn't ignore our hearts' cries, especially when they are yearnings for more of Him, a better understanding of His Word, more effective prayer, a closer relationship with Him day by day. In my confinement, the Holy Spirit was able to reach me in ways not possible while I was rushing around, dealing with the cares of this life. I began to sense the Lord more easily. We began to talk together more intimately. My Bible reading began to be exciting, and my prayer life changed. Here is an example.

I had seen miracle answers to prayer, but I also saw times when prayer seemed ineffective. There was one friend who had a problem with itching. It wasn't constant, but when it came upon her, it was maddening. She would call me to ask for prayer. Sometimes when I prayed it would go away. Sometimes, nothing changed. But one day, as I sought the Lord for more depth in prayer, He showed me a wider picture of the problem. My friend was a low-income person who always had financial worries. There were troubles with her family and she had physical issues as well. When I prayed for her itching that time, I asked the Lord to help her to trust Him in her needs. I don't remember what I said, because I ask the Lord to guide me and then I say what comes into my head. That day, apparently we identified the true source of the itching, because she told me the itching stopped shortly after the prayer. Since then, I have prayed often with her for other needs, but she has not mentioned any itching since that last time.

Jesus didn't ask people whether they were worried about bills. He just healed them. Is it important to know the root of the issue? Maybe not, though Jesus did tell one man He healed not to sin anymore, and I figure the man knew what sin the Lord was referring to. This incident showed me that sometimes the problem will not go away unless the source, the real cause, is recognized, acknowledged, and brought to the Lord in prayer.

Finally I was able to go home. All the in-home services had been set up, and a friend came in once a day to fix my breakfast and help me during the day. I am so grateful for her loving care of me. After a time, I was able to live efficiently in the new limitations in my activities, including a walker. But I was grateful for that aid, and that I was not confined to a wheelchair.

One evening as May drew near I was alone in my room not thinking about anything especially, when suddenly the Lord took my attention. He came to my mind with the question which was basically, "Will you give me your whole self?" At the same time, He showed me that I was not ready. It was so vivid in my mind. There were still things I wanted to keep. There was no hint of displeasure or punishment coming. I confessed that I was not ready, but that I wanted His help to do just that. He heard me, and since that event I have been seeking His help to turn those things over into His care.

As I thought about what had happened, I realized that was the purpose for God putting me in this place, so I could be alone with Him and spend more time getting to know Him more clearly. I could have used my time much better than I did.

Today as I write this, I find that, except for five hours a week with a caregiver and visits with my friends and family, I am still alone with God. I have learned how much He loves me, that He does take care of me over and over again. I have to, and am happy to, live day by day with His help. As I go through each day's routine I find that He is able to keep me walking with my walker. He tells me in His Word, as well as things He has given me to understand, that as His child I have everything I could need by His Spirit Who is within me. He dearly wants a close and loving relationship with every child of His. I am blessed to give Him praise and thanksgiving throughout my day. To ask questions of Him and get His answer for what to do next. It is a delightful way to live, and not a chore.

The Word of God says the same thing to every Christian. We have the totality of God by His Holy Spirit Who is His seal of our eternal soul to be with Him forever. He has given us authority over the works of Satan that we have to deal with when we are tempted, or he comes against us in his anger.

I started thinking more about who God is in his love and mercy. His love governs every thing in our lives. He has a plan for each life and what He allows to happen to us is purposed only for our good. When we realize this, it is much easier to turn ourselves over completely to follow His directions.

God has truly been more loving and faithful than I deserve, yet I can trust Him each day to keep me in His path for my life. I don't know what may come up in the future, but I have learned that with God's help and the help of family and friends I will be all right until the day He calls me Home, either in the Rapture, or on my appointed Day.

As you can see, my life has gone from one thing to another—my own physical issues, the weddings and births, departure of loved ones to heaven, family gatherings, and adjusting to the strange goings on with mysterious viruses and bizarre changes in political matters. In the midst of all these adjustments, I faced a new issue. It wasn't an emergency, and I thought it would be a small matter in my life.

I told you about the print on demand publisher who handled my book, *Forging Ahead for God.* They sold their business to another company, and that company sold to another. Now I was receiving mystifying emails about having to do things on the computer to access my book, and I had no idea what to do. But I knew

Carolyn's friend, Dan Worley, was very experienced in this area since he had done the layouts and publishing of their more than 50 books. Through him, and Carolyn's work with new, inexperienced authors whose stories God told them to publish, Earthen Vessel Productions had become a legitimate small, independent publisher. So I asked them what to do. It was February, 2021.

Carolyn suggested that I write an entirely new book. She still remembered that comment I had made at UCLA when we saw the planter full of bamboo that met Hedy's needs. I had said the supernatural Christian life is normal and told her many stories during those nights at the conference when we talked in the dark. She urged me to write a brand new book, one that tells what God has done for me and our family and close friends all through my lifetime. She thought that relating these events in a book would be a great encouragement to people in this time of uncertainty and need for God to show Himself mighty for everyday people going through trial after trial in these evil days.

I prayed about doing it. One day as I sat in my chair, the one I go to when I want to relax and talk to Jesus, I was musing the enormity of this intimidating project when all of a sudden I began getting titles—each one with a story attached. I was rather shocked. It was such a big job to write a book, but the Lord let me know that it was His plan for me. Carolyn offered to teach how to write it so stories would be as well presented as could be. When I looked at the task, however, I realized that my computer, now ancient by technological standards, was not up to the task. Once again, my dear son Steve came to the rescue. He found a computer that would do the job faster, and with much more memory than my first one. God even supplied a tech to help me with the bewildering aspects of working with electronic equipment. His name is Ron Doerksen, a godly young man I met at our prayer group. He not only helped with the hardware, he was able to translate my docs into emails for Carolyn, whose visual limitations require specific parameters so her computer can read the pages to her. Ron takes care of all of that, and is also our safeguard against accidental deletions, since he always has copies of everything. In addition, Carolyn's friend, Linda Marie, was happy to proofread and correct my manuscripts and refused to accept any money for that invaluable service.

Carolyn also offered to publish it under Earthen Vessel Productions. Of course I accepted right away. Dan quickly designed a stunning cover that represents the theme of the book and is a gorgeous photograph he took himself.

Using God's titles, I wrote each of the stories of the stunning miracles I've seen in my life. But when we had them all edited and refined, Carolyn said there needed to be one more chapter—one about my own life. She said I told everyone else's story, but this last one would be my own faith journey. I said there were no miraculous things happening in my life now, with COVID restricting travel and my age limiting my activities. Carolyn said God was doing something supernatural through this book, and the very process by which it came about is another one of my lifetime of miracles. This is why I've written so much about writing this book, and why I'm ending my story with this account of another adventure with God.

Carolyn did not tell me till much later, after I was well into the project, that God had told her He was going to use the process to bring healing for me. One of those things is the blessing that it always is to look back on one's life and see the events with new eyes, ones that notice the hand of God in them. It's not until you examine life from the perspective of lifetimes of choices and the consequences of those choices, that you begin to realize how much our individual lives matter. In the context of decades, you can see how each one's choices have their effect on those at the time and those who come after. King David is a good example. He made a lot of mistakes—really bad ones at times—but his heart was always set on his relationship with God, and the Lord blessed him with the most astonishing promise of all time: Messiah would be from his bloodline and reign forever as King. I have four grandchildren and eleven great grandchildren. They have faced their own difficulties and hard choices, and they all know how to pray. That part of the family legacy has been passed on parent to child just as it was for me and my parents before me. There is such a depth of faith in them that I am amazed. They all seem to know for certain that Jesus is listening and lovingly guiding them when they pray.

Another blessing from writing this book is seeing in new ways what God brought about through the difficulties of my life. I have always been so busy trying to tend to the needs around me that I never learned to examine the meanings of things. My parents were busy in the same way. As a pastor's wife, I did the same. I did not think to share my struggles or even victories over private concerns with my children. My parents never did, and I followed their example. And, like my parents, I did not ask my children how things were affecting them. In fact, except for the time Steve and I sat on his bed after Bob's death and I poured out my heart to him, I don't think I ever did anything like that again—with any of my children or grandchildren. In fact, I don't think I asked Steve or my other boys how they were doing or talked to them about the hurt of not having God say "yes" to our request to heal their dad. And I never even took the time to examine the impact things had on me.

This was evidenced the first time when Carolyn kept asking me how I felt when the two servicemen stood up. I told her, "Well, we were all surprised."

"Yes, but what did it mean to you?"

She did this over and over as we worked on the stories. Gradually I began to see how I was not aware of that aspect of human life. I reacted with human emotions. I cried. I rejoiced. I grieved. But I didn't go deeper or ask God for insight or understanding. I suppose, when you're in a war, you don't stop to examine what it means to you to be in the trenches. Missiles, bullets, bombs, are hitting all around you. You just react, get through it, and move on.

My dad had been someone to be good for. I adored him. He was a good man, totally trustworthy and loving, but he was often gone and he never talked about his work, his struggles or his personal relationship with God. My mother was also too busy, or maybe it never occurred to her.

When I wrote my first drafts, especially of this last chapter, it was dates and places and individuals and what happened next. Sometimes we were happy and sometimes we were sad, but where was the depth of insight that can come from such things? I never thought about them. So Carolyn prodded me. She sent emails with lists of questions, and she called and we'd talk about her questions. She observed that I contributed to my parents' ministry by being a good girl, helping with tasks, and not ever telling them my needs. I took care of those myself if I could, even as a little child. It never occurred to me to ask for a change or accommodation.

This continued into my adult years. For example, when Bob pastored the church in Monterey Park, we would get home and he would go immediately to talk to his parents about the service. I never thought to ask him to wait to see his parents until after we'd had lunch together. I simply wasn't aware that I could talk to my husband about my frustrations, and I see I've been like that with Father God as well.

The Lord has been using this chapter to transform me. He's teaching me to pour out my heart to Him. He's not just Someone to be good for. I can pray in new ways. These days are so strange…. How shall we meet them with His heart? How do we pray when some things are hideous, vile, or distorted and wicked?

When I was telling Carolyn that I wasn't having any big miracles to write about in these later years of my life, she reminded me that the most supernatural of all the aspects of the Christian life is communication with the creator of the Universe. We are meant to hear Him, receive His guidance, and share His heart. He also speaks to us through other means. She reminded me of the "writings," and of dreams and visions. I'm including one of the visions here, because it is directly related to God's course-correction and guidance as I offer myself to partner with Him for His purposes that day.

One morning I woke up early. I was snuggled and cozy in my covers, halfway between sleep and wakefulness. Unexpectedly, a picture came into my mind. I was sitting in a large auditorium with someone beside me. We were just a few rows from the front seats. No one else was there and it was dark. In the front was a large stage platform with a black stage curtain pulled all the way across it.

On the floor between the edge of the front of the stage and the rows of the seats was a wide, flat space. On it were lying quite a few pipes that looked like they were used for regular plumbing needs. There might have been 6 or 7, all of the same length but one or two shorter ones. All were lined up and looked ready for use. They were gray metal, but a few had splotches of green paint on them.

That was all there was to the picture, and I had no clue as to its meaning. I sent an email to Carolyn to find out what it might mean. She immediately began asking questions about the pipes—the paint splotches, considering the use of pipes for conveying things through walls, etc. Then she asked her friend Dan. Immediately he said that the pipes were distractions. We were there to see what was going to be performed on the stage, not to figure out what the pipes were doing there or what they were for.

Carolyn had focused on examining the pipes. She had gone to the details, the wrong part of the scene. I, too, was off track. At the time, I was intrigued with some activities of ministries that were doing secret rescues in places around the world. I was so fascinated that I spent hours on the internet reading reports of their successes. But they were distractions, like the pipes that Dan said were there to take one's eyes off whatever was going to be performed on that stage.

It was a warning to me, to focus on what God was bringing into being and not be distracted by less essential things. The stage was dark and quiet, and the pipes were interesting, but I stopped looking at the events going on in other ministries and began spending more time seeking the Lord in Bible reading and prayer. We are participants with God in this great adventure, but we will not be ready to move with Him if we are looking at other things, filling our time with them instead of Him. We are meant to make a difference. God told Carolyn "You are here to change what would be without you." Each of us is uniquely designed to change the world around us in ways only we can, but it comes from deep intimacy and communion with God, and that communion is developed as we sit, waiting, in our assigned seats, letting Him speak into the silences His own heart for our part in affecting the world.

That focus can be applied to whatever the Lord would have us do in these days of confusion, evil events, and changing circumstances, so that His work goes forward to bring our country back into righteousness and truth.

This book has been my first priority for one whole year. Now here I am, at the ending of the stories. The review of my life has been eye-opening to me in the ways God has guided me, sometimes miraculously, though it didn't seem so at the time.

He was my strength and hope in my times of difficulty and grief. His peace and love kept me on top of the problems. In my happy times He was my joy and delight so I could laugh and grow for the next trial. In every need, He was there with His solutions, every one of which was timed just right so that I did not lack any good thing.

And to you, my reader, this book has been covered in prayer that God would reveal Himself to you through the stories. The same God who did miracles for me, an older woman, an ordinary person like so many others, He will do for you when you trust Him as your Savior and give your life to Him. You will find a joy and fulfillment that you may have been seeking for a long time.

Our God is the only God. There is not another like Him. He is holy and perfect in every way. Every facet of His life is complete. There is no lack in Him. Because of that, His love can never diminish, His faithfulness can never wane, His truth will always be the same, His mercy never fails. His justice is true and will always be fair, according to the Words He has spoken in the Scriptures. And we can have an overflowing abundance of Him, which is the most amazing supernatural thing of all. A.W. Tozer said each of us has as much of Him as we want, no more, no less. I am 92, and my Lord continues to deepen and enrich my relationship with Him as I grow closer to Him, my Savior, my Comforter, my Guide, Creator, and King. My precious, beloved, ever-present Friend.

I would like to finish this book with a recent writing, "He's Coming For Us!"

HE'S COMING FOR US!

There will come a day when you will hear My voice calling you to "Come Up Higher." That will be My call for all My children to meet Me in the air and I will escort you into the realm of My Kingdom.

Your eyes and ears will be awed by the things you will see and hear—things you have longed for and tried to imagine, but could not. What you will experience will be so much more, in every way, that the grandeur of it all will be almost too much to take in.

My pleasure in watching your reactions of delight will be so fulfilling to Me, as I have so longed for this meeting to take place.

Now you are truly with Me for eternity. My Father also welcomes you with great joy, and My Spirit, with the angels will rejoice with great joy. All the saints from all the ages will be a vast crowd of loved ones eager to be among those welcoming you with open arms.

What a day that will be! Supreme Joy! All of you, worshiping Me and My Father. The hosts of Heaven will shout praises, joining you in peals of praise and rapturous Hallelujahs.

No longer will you battle the enemy, or bear the loss of loved ones, or feel sickness and pain. Any tears will be tears of joy that overflow. You are finally free from all evil, to live in total freedom to praise and worship Me forever.

Are you ready to hear My call? Are you expecting to hear it? You must make every effort to be ready now, for My call to gather you will be so quick there will be no time for any preparations.

Examine yourselves now to be sure you are in the faith (2 Cor. 13:5). Deal with anything idolatrous—anything that would cause you to look back as you leave. Check with My Holy Spirit to identify anything you need to confess, anyone you need to forgive, anything that interrupts your connection with Me, and clear it all so that you will be certain to hear My call to "Come Up Higher."

That call is coming soon. Don't miss it, for I can't wait to greet you in the air! Amen!

Inspiration given to
Darda Burkhart, 3/26/19

www.ingramcontent.com/pod-product-compliance
Lightning Source LLC
LaVergne TN
LVHW051059080426
835508LV00019B/1973